THE AUTOBIOGRAPHY
OF ŌSUGI SAKAE

VOICES FROM ASIA

THE
AUTOBIOGRAPHY
OF
ŌSUGI
SAKAE

TRANSLATED WITH ANNOTATIONS BY
BYRON K. MARSHALL

UNIVERSITY OF CALIFORNIA PRESS
Berkeley • Los Angeles • Oxford

University of California Press
Berkeley and Los Angeles, California

University of California Press, Ltd.
Oxford, England

Partial funding for the project was provided by the Sasakawa Peace Foundation
and The Pacific Basin Institute.

Library of Congress Cataloging-in-Publication Data

Ōsugi, Sakae, 1885–1923.
   [Jijoden. English]
   The autobiography of Ōsugi Sakae / translated with annotations by
Byron K. Marshall.
      p.   cm. — (Voices from Asia; 6)
   Translation of: Jijoden.
   Includes bibliographical references.
   ISBN 0-520-07759-8. — ISBN 0-520-07760-1 (paper)
   1. Ōsugi, Sakae, 1885–1923. 2. Anarchists—Japan—Biography.
I. Title. II. Series.
HX947.Z67076413 1992
335′ .83′092—dc20
   [B]
                              91-31015
                                  CIP

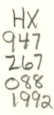

Printed in the United States of America
9 8 7 6 5 4 3 2 1

The paper used in this publication meets the minimum requirements
of American National Standard for Information Sciences—Permanence
of Paper for Printed Library Materials, ANSI Z39.48-1984. ♾

Dedicated to
the *onshi*
of my formative years
at Stanford

CONTENTS

ACKNOWLEDGMENTS

This project originated many years ago when I was a master of arts candidate in the Department of Asian Languages at Stanford University, and this volume is thus dedicated to the teachers of that period.

Professor Thomas C. Smith, then in the Stanford history department, originally suggested the desirability of a translation of Ōsugi's *Autobiography*. After completing one version of the work, I turned from it to a study of one of Ōsugi's predecessors, Nakae Chōmin, and later to their antagonists among the elites of business and academia. More recently, though, Thomas Smith again encouraged me to return to Ōsugi. The late Robert Brower, then also on the Stanford faculty, was the departmental advisor who shepherded the original version through the master's degree process. Returning to that first version, I have reworked most of the translation, added the material in chapter 7, and revised all the annotations. But if the finished product has any merit, it remains partially to the credit of William Naff. Long before becoming an award-winning translator at the University of Massachusetts, Bill tutored me on translation that year at Stanford; he bears no responsibility for flaws in the present version. On the faculty at that same time were William McCullough and Frank Motofuji, who were always willing to help, as was Hiroshi Miyaji, then a fellow graduate assistant.

I also wish to acknowledge debts to several others directly involved at later stages: Betsey Scheiner, who enthusiastically undertook to oversee the project; Fred Notehelfer, Pamela MacFarland Holway, Edith Gladstone, and an anonymous reader for the University of California Press, who saved me from even more embarrassing faux pas than still remain in this version; my wife; the grants committee of the Graduate School and those other colleagues here at the University of Minnesota who sometimes tolerated my preoccupation with this work at the expense of other priorities.

B. K. M.
Minneapolis, 1991

TRANSLATOR'S INTRODUCTION

ŌSUGI AS A MODERN JAPANESE REBEL

Ōsugi Sakae was a central figure in the left-wing radicalism of early twentieth-century Japan. Labeled a "pioneer of freedom" and "the shogun of anarchism," he was admired by some of his fellow Japanese before and by many more after World War II for his rebellion against an overbearing state and an oppressive society.

Ōsugi became a political activist while a student of only nineteen. Two years later, in 1906, he was arrested in a street demonstration protesting the economic oppression of the working class. This led to his first prison sentence at the age of twenty-one. He would be arrested three more times in the next two years alone, serving a total of almost thirty-six months in prison before he was twenty-seven years old. This government suppression, when combined with factional disputes within the radical movement and its inability to attract popular support, halted the momentum of the political left. After the 1910 show trials that condemned to death such prominent activists as Kanno Sugako and Kōtoku Shūsui for plotting the assassination of the emperor, even the nonviolent left was forced into a period of near dormancy.

By the time the movement reawakened at the end of the First World War, Ōsugi had reaped a certain notoriety from a 1916 scandal involv-

ing two of the most famous women radicals of the day, Kamichika
Ichiko and Itō Noe. Concurrent adulterous affairs with the two women
led to a published denunciation by his wife, who then divorced him, and
to a sensational trial for Kamichika, who spent two years in prison for
assaulting Ōsugi with a knife. It was this scandal, as much as his essays
on free love, that earned him the sobriquet of "the erotic anarchist."

But Ōsugi had also established a more serious reputation as an
editor, essayist, and translator. In part because of his translations of
Kropotkin, he became known as "the leading anarchist thinker of this
period" and a "charismatic" theorist for the then dynamic anarcho-
syndicalist wing of the labor movement.[1] Ōsugi was also the main Japanese representative at the 1920 conference of Far Eastern Socialists
held in Shanghai under the auspices of the Comintern. The Communists
were initially willing to provide funds for Ōsugi's efforts, but his subsequent estrangement from bolshevism and the growing strength of
more moderate Japanese labor leaders meant that Ōsugi was gradually
to lose political influence.

In 1922 Ōsugi set off with a false passport to visit Europe and confer
with the Western anarchists who had invited him. On May Day 1923
French police arrested him as he spoke at a rally in the suburbs of Paris
and deported him to Japan, perhaps at the request of Japanese authorities. He had only two more months to live. His death in September
came at the hands of members of the military police who had kidnapped
him along with his second wife, Itō Noe, and a six-year-old nephew during the chaotic aftermath of the devastating Kantō earthquake of 1923.

Ōsugi is thus celebrated as an early twentieth-century rebel who left
a legacy of struggle against the establishment, even though he achieved
little in the way of concrete political or social reforms in his own time.
The brutal circumstances of his death transformed Ōsugi into a martyr
at the age of thirty-eight, neutralizing some of his critics and perhaps
sparing him the ignominy that attached to those comrades who eventually strayed from the cause. But what sets Ōsugi apart from his fellow

1. Stephen S. Large, *Organized Workers and Socialist Politics in Interwar Japan*, 32;
Tatsuo Arima, *The Failure of Freedom*, 60. For more on Ōsugi's influence, see other
works on the socialist movement and Thomas Stanley's very informative biography,
Ōsugi Sakae, listed in the bibliography.

radicals is not merely that he was once in the forefront of the movement, or even that his life had such dramatic elements. His flamboyant personality and flair for the dramatic were almost matched by his skill as a writer. Throughout his adult life Ōsugi supported himself by editing and contributing to a variety of leftist periodicals. The first posthumous publication of his complete works, including one work of fiction co-authored with Itō Noe, ran to nine good-size volumes in the late 1920s; postwar versions reached fourteen. These translations and original works, including the *Autobiography,* earned Ōsugi a secure place in both the socialist canon and the history of the development of what is known as "proletarian literature" in Japan.[2]

Ōsugi's *Autobiography* can thus be read on several levels. Chapters 5 and 6 offer a view inside the fledgling socialist movement around the time of the Russo-Japanese War. Here he reminisces about meetings of the Commoners Society (Heiminsha) in 1904 and friction within the loose coalition of Marxists, labor unionists, and Christian socialists who agitated for social reform at home and pacifism abroad. He also analyzes the influences that led him to commit irreversibly to the movement. Chapter 7 describes the months and years in prisons that many others in the movement also endured. At this level, the significance of the *Autobiography* as historical document is clear.

Ōsugi himself clearly intended that the earlier chapters also be read for insights about the formative years of a rebel. For many readers these insights will be the best justification for an English translation. Chapters 1 through 3 describe a childhood and adolescence circumscribed by the narrow horizons of an army family posted to a garrison town, although we also glimpse the opulent life-style of the military elite when Ōsugi visits his Tokyo relatives. Always Ōsugi is at pains to show us how little freedom was possible in this brutalizing atmosphere, as in chapter 4 when he takes us to the dormitories and playing fields of the military education system.[3] The leitmotif throughout is personal freedom—how

2. See, for example, Yamada Seizaburō, ed., *Puroretaria bungakushi.*
3. Some of the violence and sexual behavior Ōsugi depicts has analogues in the boarding schools for the civilian elite; see Donald T. Roden, *Schooldays in Imperial Japan* and my review in *Journal of Japanese Studies* 8, no. 1 (Winter 1982): 205–8.

possession or deprivation of it determines the development of individuals and their relations with others.

Although the entire work expresses this perspective, it also contains extraordinarily compelling descriptions of Meiji life that go beyond the historical significance of Ōsugi as a radical thinker or of the political movement in which he participated. There are, for instance, rare sketches of life in a provincial town far from the modernizing Tokyo or Osaka. Among its most sympathetic inhabitants were the schoolgirls, army wives, and other females Ōsugi portrays in considerable detail. And, although we cannot easily assess how typical his experiences were, he offers interesting scenes of the highly competitive environment of the school system there, as well as in Tokyo of the 1900s. In contrast to such schools, the military academies matriculated only a small minority of Japanese youths, but even fewer had Ōsugi's skill or reason to write an exposé. The result translated here may well be unique.

Throughout, Ōsugi reminds us that sharp contrasts characterize his life. He begins this account by describing the surprise expressed by a prison guard that Ōsugi of all people should have come to such a place. His family held quite conventional attitudes: his father was a decorated officer who served in both of Meiji Japan's triumphant wars; his mother was a spirited but nonetheless dutiful army wife with no apparent aspirations other than those for her family. The public elementary and middle school that Ōsugi attended stressed the values of patriotic duty and obedience to authority, while his peers enforced the collective norms of informal youth gangs—all of which prepared him for a military education. Yet he subtly foreshadows what many of his readers would already know: his subsequent rejection of these conventions and the success of his rebellious spirit in withstanding even the rigors of imprisonment.

The tone that dominates Ōsugi's account of his life, however, is not acrimony but irony. If the vignettes of authority figures are sharply pointed, Ōsugi's animosity is frequently tempered by a poignant humor and a wry wit. If he dwells on the oppressive aspects of his early life, it is also true that he crafts his memoirs with an ear for telling dialogue and a sure dramatic touch. And throughout the indictment of his soci-

ety, he sustains a lucid prose style. These characteristics no doubt partially explain the popularity of the work among Japanese readers;
they—rather than any inherent difficulties in the vocabulary or syntax—
also constitute the main challenge to the translator.

A NOTE ON TEXTS

The *Autobiography* (*Jijōden*) first appeared serially in the influential
magazine *Kaizō* between September 1921 and January 1922; but it is
only a part of Ōsugi's autobiographical writings. In 1919 he had published a series of short pieces on his prison experiences, *Prison Memoirs*
(*Gokuchūki*); it is usually included as chapter 7 of the *Autobiography*,
as here. Another piece often included was published two years earlier as
a separate entity entitled "The Hayama Affair" (*Hayama jiken*). It deals
with the stabbing incident that took place six years after the last event
in the autobiography. In it Ōsugi clearly indicated his intention to fill in
the intervening years, a project that his murder prevented.[4] I do not include that piece here.

For the most part I use the 1930 Kaizōsha edition of the autobiography. It offered the advantage of complete *furigana* glosses—that is,
phonetic syllabary printed alongside the Chinese characters to indicate
pronunciation—at times very helpful if not necessarily authoritative.
This version was subjected to government censorship and therefore rep-
resents the text usually available to readers before the Second World
War. Its censors employed the *fuseji* technique; that is, they substituted
an X, an O, or some other mark for each printed character they deleted.[5] Quite often—but by no means always—the reader would have
been able to fill in the blanks with the same ease as in the case of deleted
expletives in English-language texts. The 1961 edition published by
Gendai Shisō Sha restored most of the censored passages without indi-
cating the source of its additions. Wherever I am confident of the sense
in such passages, I restore words or phrases and put them in brackets.

---

4. A later travel diary, *Nihon datsu shukki*, covered his 1923 trip to Europe.
5. See Richard H. Mitchell, *Censorship in Imperial Japan*, 161 ff.; and Jay Rubin,
Injurious to Public Morals, 29–31.

The *Autobiography* was republished after the Second World War and included in the prestigious 1957 Chikuma Publishing Company series on contemporary literature. I do not attempt to address the question of authoritative texts. Those interested in such matters will find relevant citations in the bibliography. My concern here is less with the author's original intent than with the meaning that has been accessible to the largest Japanese audience. By the same token, whenever faced with a choice between a literal but perhaps unintelligible rendering and a loose but credible sense of a passage, I have chosen to be impaled on the latter horn of the translator's dilemma.

To the best of my knowledge there is no other translation into English of any substantial portions of the *Autobiography* or any other of Ōsugi's voluminous writings, although Thomas A. Stanley has excerpted many passages for his biography, *Ōsugi Sakae: Anarchist in Taishō Japan*. Given the existence of this biography in English, I do not clutter this translation with an abundance of annotations, limiting them to pertinent information necessary to add to the understanding of readers totally unused to Meiji Japan. Most place-names mentioned in the text can be found quite easily on any good map of Japan.

A NOTE ON MECHANICS

All dates of events and references to ages of individuals are left as in the original. Since the text does not usually give the year of an event, for the readers' convenience I add approximate dates to the chapter titles and provide a brief chronology at the end of the introduction. In the case of ages, readers should remember that by the Japanese reckoning an individual turns two years old on the first New Year's Day following his or her birth and by Western reckoning would thus often be a year younger. Japan was not yet on the metric system in this period and most of the measurements are given in the old-fashioned units. Here I usually render them into their American counterparts, using the metric system only where Ōsugi chose to.

Except for well known place-names, diacritics signifying long vowels are essential in romanizing Japanese and are indicated here with Ō, ō, and *ū*. The usage followed is generally that in the *Kenkyusha New Japanese-English Dictionary* (or, for some proper nouns, the *Kodansha Encyclopedia of Japan*) — of italicizing terms other than proper nouns or words in common use in English. Names of Japanese individuals are here always given with the family names first. Writers and political activists in the Meiji period not uncommonly had one or even more noms de plume or noms de guerre. In this I follow Ōsugi's text but give alternatives in the notes, which also explain other potential confusions.

CHRONOLOGY OF MAJOR EVENTS IN *THE AUTOBIOGRAPHY*

1885
   Birth in Marugame in Kagawa Prefecture (January)

1889   (AGE 4)
   Move to Shibata in Niigata Prefecture (winter)

1891   (AGE 6)
   Entrance to lower elementary school (spring)

1894   (AGE 9)
   Father in Sino-Japanese War (until March 1895)

1895   (AGE 10)
   Entrance to upper elementary school (spring)

1897   (AGE 12)
   Entrance to Shibata Middle School (autumn)

1899   (AGE 14)
   Entrance to Nagoya Military Cadet School (spring)

1901   (AGE 16)
   Expulsion from military school (November)

1902   (AGE 17)
   Attendance at Tōkyō Gakuin and, at night, the French Language School
      (January)
   Death of mother in Niigata (June)
   Entrance to Junten Middle School in Tokyo (October)

1903   (AGE 18)
   Entrance to Foreign Language College in Tokyo; founding of *Commoners
      News* (*Heimin Shimbun*) (September)

1904   (AGE 19)
Outbreak of Russo-Japanese War (February)

1906   (AGE 21)
Arrest in Tokyo Streetcar Fare Incident (March)
Marriage to Hori Yasuko, sister-in-law of Sakai Toshihiko (September)
Indictment for violating the Press Ordinance (November)

1907   (AGE 22)
Arrest for violating the Press Ordinance (March)

1908   (AGE 23)
Arrest in Rooftop Speech Incident (January)
Arrest in Red Flags Incident in Tokyo (March)

1909   (AGE 24)
In Sugamo Prison

1910   (AGE 25)
Release from prison (November)
Announcement of death sentence against Kōtoku Shūsui and others
   (December)

1914   (AGE 29)
Start of affair with Kamichika Ichiko (1888–1981) (autumn)

1916   (AGE 31)
Start of affair with Itō Noe (1895–1923)
Attack by Kamichika in the Hikage Teahouse Incident (November)

1919   (AGE 34)
First publication of *Prison Memoirs* (January–April)

1921   (AGE 37)
First serial publication of his autobiography in the magazine *Kaizō*
   (September–January 1922)

1922   (AGE 38)
Departure for anarchist meetings in Europe (December)

1923   (AGE 39)
Arrest in Paris and deportation to Japan (May)
Murder by members of the military police (September)

SOURCE: Nishida Masaru, "Ōsugi Sakae nenpu"; appendix to *Ōsugi Sakae Zenshū;*
Thomas A. Stanley, *Ōsugi Sakae,* xv–xviii. Ages are given here in Western reckoning.

THE AUTOBIOGRAPHY
OF ŌSUGI SAKAE

FIRST
MEMORIES
TO 1894

I.

It was the morning of the second or third day after we had been arrested for the Red Flags Incident.[1] We had been taken first to Tokyo Jail and then to Chiba Prison. Now for the first time all of those who had been brought in together were led out into a central courtyard for exercise. The yard was between the wings of the building—a rather large dreary open area surfaced with cinders so that not a blade of grass grew.

We lined up and the prison sergeant in charge unrolled a list, slowly checking each of our faces against the names and descriptions. Suddenly he frowned and looked back and forth from my face to the list, checking and rechecking as if puzzled. Then, staring down his nose at me, he

1. In this *Akahata jiken* of June 1908, Ōsugi was arrested and subsequently sentenced to two and one-half years in prison for violating the Peace Preservation Law. Following a meeting to celebrate the release from prison of a prominent Socialist—Yamaguchi Gizō (also known as Kaizō or Koken [1883–1920])—Ōsugi and others began to sing revolutionary songs and wave large red flags emblazoned with slogans such as "Anarchism" and "Communism." Among the dozen demonstrators arrested were Arahata Kanson (1887–1981), Sakai Toshihiko (1870–1933), and Yamaguchi; three who later helped found the Japanese Communist party. Also arrested was Kanno Sugako (1881–1911), the female activist who would die on the gallows in 1911 for plotting to assassinate the emperor. Ōsugi's various terms in prison are recounted in chapter 7.

asked in a slightly nasal northeastern accent, "You—you're related some way to Ōsugi Azuma, aren't you?"

I was certain that next to my name on the list was the information, "eldest son of Azuma." To go to the trouble of asking, the guard must be someone who knew of my father. Since he looked to be in his thirties and seemed unusually alert for a prison official, and because of the friendly tone in his voice, I wondered if he hadn't perhaps once served as a noncommissioned officer in the regiment in Echigo. I thought to myself, Sergeant, you must be surprised to see the old man's name connected with a prison record like mine! Rather than answer him, I simply grinned. It was a little unsettling in these circumstances to meet someone who had known my father.

"Don't you know someone named Azuma?" he asked again suspiciously. "Ōsugi Azuma, the army officer?"

When I continued to stand there grinning in silence, Sakai[2] broke in and answered for me: "How could he not know? That's Ōsugi's old man."

"So—I was right. I served under him when he was a battalion commander. Hmm, so this is the son of the ol' Idealist," he said half to himself as if distracted by his own thoughts. Then, returning to me, "Ōsugi was famous in the Second Division for being an idealist. How's it his son would end up in a place like this?"

The term "idealist" was an army cliché meaning loyal, patriotic, devoted to the military spirit. It was a term of respect but carried overtones of "stiff," "unbending," and not overly strong on military strategy.

When I had come home after being expelled from the military cadet school, many people remarked in surprise that my father was "such a gentleman." At the time someone who seemed to know my family better said in my defense, "Well, you don't know his mother." Actually I don't really know which I am more like, my father or my mother, but I certainly looked more like Mother.

2. Sakai Toshihiko, an influential journalist and pioneer socialist. A co-founder of the *Heimin Shimbun* (Commoners News) and of the Japanese Socialist party (in 1906), Sakai was arrested as a result of the Red Flags Incident and sentenced to two years in prison. At the time Ōsugi was married to the sister of Sakai's wife, but she divorced Ōsugi before his autobiography was published.

"Does he really look so much like me?" she would ask people. And then, gently pinching my nose, "But I don't have such a horrible nose!" My mother was pretty; her nose was high and straight whereas mine was flat and lumpy at the tip.

I was told that when my father became a second lieutenant in the Imperial Guards his battalion commander, Colonel Yamada, was selecting a husband for his wife's younger sister. Though there were two candidates, in the end the prize went to my father.

My mother, who was living with the Yamadas at the time, was quite a tomboy. When Yamada's horse was saddled and left in front of the house for him, Mother would often climb on and gallop the horse up and down the yard.

Once my younger brother Noburu and I were discussing our relatives, when he said, "I've heard our grandfather on Mother's side was quite an interesting fellow. I heard a lot about him from Yone in Osaka, but I was so fascinated listening to him I didn't try to remember any of it. Maybe you take after grandfather." And he urged me to ask our cousin Yone about it when I had a chance. Until then, of the relatives on my mother's side I knew only the sister who was married to Yamada, the next youngest sister who was Yone's mother, and my grandmother. I had never heard a thing about my grandfather or so much as given him a thought. Since my grandmother was an extremely uncouth individual, I dismissed the whole idea, thinking that my mother's family was probably not altogether respectable.

Still, since Yone and a comrade of mine in Osaka knew each other and I understood that they often spoke of me, I was inclined to feel somewhat closer to Yone. Thus when I was in Osaka I finally went to see Yone. He had inherited my grandfather's house and had a shoe shop near Yodoyabashi. I was just twenty when I met him.

"Do you recognize me?" I asked Yone as soon as I entered the shop. I had just given the slip to a man tailing me and I didn't want Yone's clerks to know my name.[3]

---

3. Although the text is not explicit here, Ōsugi was no doubt under police surveillance. Because of such police harassment, especially during the Russo-Japanese War, the socialist leaders depended greatly on students who could travel the country less conspicuously to disseminate their literature and gather subscriptions to their periodicals. Ōsugi

"Of course I do. No one except my family has eyes like those," he replied with exaggeration, staring at me with eyes even larger than mine. He then led me into the rear of the shop.

My grandfather's name was Kusui Rikimatsu. He was from near Minato-nana-maguri in Wakayama, where I understand he had a rather large sake brewery. From his youth he had been very strong and quite a rogue. When this grandfather was twelve, one of the domain's martial arts instructors, a man named Date, picked him as a pupil and Grandfather became his apprentice. By the time Grandfather was eighteen he had received his certificate of proficiency. He was well versed in judo, swordsmanship, horsemanship, and use of the lance. He made judo his particular specialty and eventually opened a judo academy under the sponsorship of Date. It had five hundred day students and one hundred boarders.

Grandfather was a huge man, six feet four inches and 350 pounds. They say that even when he died at the age of thirty-three he still weighed 300 pounds. Yone had many stories about him.

"Once, probably during some holiday festival, the samurai and the townspeople had an argument over some trivial matter. Grandfather became angry and finally exchanged heated words with a large group of samurai. From that time on he was the sworn enemy of all samurai and always stood up for the townspeople. That was the cause of our family's ruin." Yone always tended to glorify our grandfather and the stories made such fascinating listening that, like my brother, I could never remember them afterward.

My father's home was near the town of Tsushima, ten miles west of Nagoya, in a place called Ōaza-Uji that was part of the administrative village of Koshiji. Now Koshiji has been merged with another village to form Kamimori. It seems that my father's family usually served as headmen of Uji. There is a story that the name Ōsugi became our family

---

had been helping at the *Heimin Shimbun* since 1904; he was probably in Osaka that year on some such mission but the police had marked him. By Western reckoning he was nineteen.

name because of a large tree at the place.[4] A certain lord out hunting with his falcon passed by and, admiring the tree, exclaimed, "What a huge cryptomeria that is!" Though this is not a very reliable story, even now a tall cryptomeria does stand there just off the main road as if it were a guidepost.

This grandfather died while my father was overseas in the Sino-Japanese War.[5] Because of his death the school in Uji was forced to close for one day. I don't recall hearing anything else about this grandfather except that his name was something like Tenkurō or Tenshiichirō.

Near Kiyosu lived an old man named Niwa something who was my grandfather's younger brother. He had a small reputation as a scholar of nativist studies.[6] We still have the inkstone and water jar he used for mixing ink. When I went to Nagoya at fifteen to enter military cadet school, my father had me stop and visit him. My father also had two elder brothers. The older, Inoko, inherited the house in Uji and served as headman. The next one, Kazumasa, lived in Nagoya. While I was at cadet school he was quite kind to me, yet I never understood what he did for a living. He went to the courthouse quite often, it seemed; I wondered if he wasn't a moneylender. I don't know how much property my grandfather left them, but it was divided between these two uncles and my father. Uncle Inoko managed my father's share. But Uncle tried his hand at several enterprises and, when they failed, my father's share was lost too. "If we had it now," my mother often complained, "we could easily have paid the school expenses for two or three of you children." I think it was probably because of this that my father never took much interest in Uncle Inoko's affairs. Nor did he pay much more attention to Uncle Kazumasa.

It seemed the Yamadas were the only people with whom my parents had a relationship such as true relatives have. The Yamadas had a con-

4. The Chinese characters for Ōsugi mean "large cryptomeria tree."

5. The Japanese and the Chinese armies fought in Korea and Manchuria between July 1894 and March 1895.

6. *Kokugaku* or "national learning" involved literary, religious, and, eventually, political scholarship that stressed ancient traditions believed to predate Chinese Confucian or Buddhist influences. In this period its teachings formed the core of a very influential strain of emperor-centered nationalism.

siderable influence on me, and my name, Sakae, was taken from a reading of one of the Chinese characters in my aunt's name. Yet you cannot fight against inheritance. Inoko and Kazumasa both stuttered, as did the old man Niwa. My father stuttered some. And, as you might expect, I have always been a stutterer.

II.

My father had no formal schooling. Yet from childhood he liked to read and often borrowed books from Niwa. As was the local custom for third sons, my father entered a Buddhist temple and was for a time a priest. The Satsuma Rebellion broke out, however, and my father began to have higher ambitions.[7] He soon ran away from the temple and went to the capital, Tokyo. First he joined a training unit and became a noncommissioned officer; then, after more study, he finally entered the officer training school. Shortly after he became a second lieutenant he married my mother and was assigned to the regiment in Marugame.

It was there that I was born. I don't recall the address or the name of the neighborhood. In the official family register my birth date is given as 17 May 1885, but I understand the date was actually 17 January. At that time company-grade officers were practically prohibited from marrying. If they did, they had to post a guaranty fee of three hundred yen. Since my father could not afford to pay, he did not apply to have the marriage registered until it was certain my mother was pregnant. My birth date was thus recorded as later than it was in fact.

Before long my father returned to the Imperial Guards in Tokyo. Then, when I was five and my parents had three children on their hands, he was transferred to Shibata in Echigo province, where he remained in obscurity for fourteen years. Because I was raised there until I was fifteen, Shibata is almost my hometown and my memories really begin there.[8] But I do remember a little about the period we lived in Tokyo.

7. In 1877 Saigō Takamori (1828–1877), one of the greatest heroes of the Meiji Restoration, led some 40,000 Satsuma and other samurai into battle against his former colleagues in the Tokyo government. What may have inspired Ōsugi's father was the new recognition given the modern-style army when it proved itself victorious against Saigō's samurai. In chapter 3 part 4 Ōsugi mentions his youthful admiration for Saigō.

8. As late as 1910 this former castle town had fewer than 12,000 inhabitants and was more than 27 kilometers from the nearest city, Niigata, the prefectural capital, which itself had a population of only 59,000.

The house was somewhere in Banchō. There was a house on either side of a gate and our house was behind them. In one of the houses next to the gate lived a little girl named Oyone. If I remember correctly, she was a year older than I. We were great friends. I was still too young for school but she was already going to kindergarten and beginning to learn songs. When she came home she would practice them in a loud voice, which made me furious since I didn't know any songs. So whenever I heard her singing in the house across the way, I would shout over and over with all my might some nonsense like "Rain—kon! Kon! Snow—kon! Kon!"

In the spring of my fifth year I began kindergarten and set off every day to Fujimi Elementary School holding Oyone's hand. Actually I can't say for certain it was the kindergarten affiliated with Fujimi School, but once later when I passed by I recalled having seen it before. I went inside to look; it was just as I had always remembered my kindergarten. Therefore I decided on my own that it must have been this school. I recall hardly anything that happened in kindergarten except that once I think I was scolded by a woman teacher and I spat in her face. Possibly all I really remember is my mother telling the story afterward. Another time later, I do recall making an elementary schoolteacher cry by spitting at her.

The regiment in which my father was serving was stationed at the Aoyama parade grounds. When it was his turn to stay on the post he would be away from home for a week or so. One day—probably the third or fourth day he had been gone—I grew very lonely for him. I and this same Oyone ran away to go to Aoyama. Just as we reached the entrance to the parade grounds Oyone burst into tears, saying she couldn't walk another step. At the same moment a dog began to bark at us. I also started to cry. We were calmed by a passing soldier and finally taken to my father.

I understand that usually an officer is posted to the regiment in Shibata as an exile for having committed some blunder. Indeed, it is probably true that anyone sent to one of those remote posts in the countryside is sent for that reason. Once, long after we had arrived in Shibata, a group of officers gathered at our home and my father treated them to some cigars my Aunt Yamada had sent from Tokyo. None of them knew how to smoke a cigar—they all put the wrong end in their mouth; Shibata was that far out in the country. I don't know what my father had done to be sent to Shibata but I heard that once, on some occasion when he was on duty at the emperor's palace, Father's horse threw him and he landed in the moat. As he was climbing out covered with mud the emperor saw him and laughed in delight: "Look, a monkey! a monkey!" But doubtless that would have been an honor for my father, not a cause for loss of face. Actually, my father did look a little like a monkey.

In any case, my father was banished to Shibata. We left Tokyo with another junior officer who was also being sent there. The only thing I remember of that trip was crossing Usui Pass. The cog railway had not yet been built at the pass and we rode in two rickety horse carriages, miles above sea level. The other officer had three in his family and they rode in one carriage. We rode in the other, my father and mother each holding one of my sisters on a lap. I sat by myself, holding on tightly. The carriage frequently lurched as if it would turn over. When we looked down, a thick fog hid the bottom of the gorge hundreds of feet below. Time after time I felt frightened almost to death.

Recently, preparing to write this autobiography, I went to visit Shibata for the first time in twenty years. Ten or fifteen years ago the railroad was completed and a station built. I went expecting things to be so changed that it would be almost completely different. I was surprised: nearly everything looked just as it had twenty years before. As soon as I got off the train, I left the station and when I saw the towering silk mill—looking like a high-class jail—I had the feeling that the flood tide of the industrial revolution had swept over Shibata too. I was wrong. I walked all around the town and, except for the silk mill, not a single thing resembled a factory. Shibata was still as much an army town as ever—a town barely managing to make a living off the troops.

The silk mill belonged to Ōkura Kihachirō and had a large sign reading Ōkura Silk Mills. The mill had been built more for the sake of satisfying Ōkura's vanity than for bringing him profits. Ōkura was born in Shibata. The story is that he failed in business and, owing everybody in the neighborhood money, left town in the middle of the night carrying his only possessions in a bundle on the end of a stick. That same Ōkura later became a millionaire and a baron.[9] He returned to Shibata to build a silk mill in his hometown and to erect a bronze statue of himself in the compound of the Suwa Shrine, next door to the mill. In terms of morality, the tide of capitalism had reached Shibata. The bronze statue of himself was Ōkura's own doing, but the townspeople themselves went so far as to display Ōkura's portrait conspicuously in the auditorium of the elementary school.

Our family moved often and we lived in a dozen or so different houses in Shibata. Although three or four of them suffered fires, the rest were almost exactly as they had been years ago. I went to visit each of them, following the same order we had lived in them.

The first house was still standing, but I recalled nothing about it. The second had not burned either. I remember setting out for elementary school from this house, so I must have been seven or eight at the time. Next door was a carpenter named Okawa Hatsu. He had a son a year or two older than I and a daughter a year or two younger. The three of us were friends. My memories about this place were not about these two, however. They were about another friend—a girl who lived five or six hundred yards away. I will probably mention her again more than once but for the time being I'll just call her Mitsuko.

Mitsuko and I were in the same grade in school and for some reason or another I was infatuated with her. Since our families had no contact with each other and we lived in different neighborhoods, there was no way of getting to know each other. Every time I happened to pass near her in school she was always unkind in one way or another. One day I was sitting at home when suddenly I very badly wanted to see her face. I went outside and came across the Okawa girl. Without warning I slapped her and grabbed the lacquered comb she wore in her hair.

9. Ōkura (1835–1928), mentioned again in chapters 3 and 6, was a former samurai who became one of the most prominent businessmen of the Meiji era. Ōkura first made his fortune through selling guns to the early Meiji government and then provisioned the military in the wars with China and with Russia; he was also later involved with the South Manchurian Railway Company and Japanese economic expansion on the continent. Evidently Ōsugi considered him the archetype of Japanese capitalist.

Clutching the comb in my hand, I ran all the way to Mitsuko's house. There she was in the front playing. I threw the comb at her feet and ran home as fast as my legs would carry me.

The third house was at the end of a block called San-no-maru, right next to the elementary school. The school had been remodeled and completely changed. The house, although listing considerably to one side, had been preserved just as it was thirty years ago. I lingered awhile in front of the gate, staring in the window of a room just to the left of the front door. It once was my room. Since the shutters had been left open, I could see through into the sitting room. There were usually sliding shoji screens between the two rooms and my memory was fixed on those paper screens. I have forgotten what it was I had done—probably I had been playing with matches—but my mother scolded me soundly. In a fit of anger I then set the paper shoji on fire and they burst immediately into flame. My mother shouted for the maid and the two of them tore down the shoji and, after considerable confusion, managed to extinguish the fire.

I walked across the street to the schoolroom where I had spent the fourth grade. As I gazed about, I was almost trembling with excitement. The teacher in charge was named Mr. Shima. He was not much more than twenty years old, and resembled a dwarf. He used to shut his mouth tightly, eyes glittering with malice, and bring his bamboo pointer down with a crack on the top of the desk. If any students talked in class, he hit them with it. Nearly every day I cowered beneath that pointer. Though I don't recall the circumstances, it was thanks to that teacher that I hated arithmetic. Five or six years afterward, when I was in Tokyo on summer vacation from military cadet school, I ran into him unexpectedly. His mouth was tightly closed and he looked as ill-tempered as ever. Much shorter than I and rather shabbily dressed, he looked more like a student houseboy than a teacher.

I recall another instructor at the school: an older man named Saitō who was my second- or third-grade teacher. He was always making eyes at the girls in class and guffawing with his big mouth wide open. He did nothing but play around with the girls, continually putting his arm around Mitsuko and others while laughing his cackling laugh. If you pulled some prank, he took you into one of the girls' classrooms as punishment and made you stand at the front, facing the whole class while holding a teapot full of water in your hands. Your back would be to the teacher; I used to take advantage of this to tease the class, rolling my eyes and sticking out my tongue. There was a teachers' room next to the classrooms and, on the other side of that, a storeroom. I can't count the number of times I was made to stay after school in the teachers' room. Sometimes I was even locked in the pitch-dark storeroom. Inside were piled old desks and chairs. After your eyes gradually became used to the dark, you could see the rats scampering about the floor. When I was kept there too long I would get bored and sometimes just emptied my bowels in the middle of the floor.

It was the janitors, not the teachers, who took care of us when we had problems. There were two of them: one short and always smiling, the other tall with a rough, frightening face. When they had time to themselves, they would sit in front of the iron kettle on the large hearth in the custodians' room and work on fishing nets. I went there often to be pampered after being scolded by one of the teachers. I always listened closely to whatever they had to say.

III.

At school I was punished or scolded almost every day by the teachers. I was also constantly disciplined at home. It was as if my mother's chief duty each day was to spank me or shout at me. Mother had a loud voice and it was seldom silent. It was so loud that people who came to visit always knew whether she was at home or not before they even entered the front gate. When she was scolding me, her voice became even louder. The way she scolded was ridiculous. Though I always stuttered, she would grab me and shout, "You're stuttering again!" Being an impatient woman, she could not bear to watch me batting my eyes and working my mouth without saying something about it. Nor could she stand my stammering "da-da-da . . ." when I was trying to talk. I don't know how many times she boxed my ears, shouting "You're stuttering again!"

Whenever I heard her call my name in that loud voice I was sure she had found out about some mischief I had done and would come to her reluctantly. "Bring the broom! Bring the broom!" she would shout. And having no choice I would go to the kitchen to get the long-handled bamboo broom. "This child is really stupid," she used to say to her bosom friend, Mrs. Tani, while patting me on the head.

"When I call for the broom he always brings it, knowing full well he's going to get a beating with it. Then he hands it to me and stands there with a blank look on his face, despite the fact he'd be better off trying to run away. That just makes it worse and all the more the reason to spank him, doesn't it?"

"Even so, a broom is cruel, don't you think?" Mrs. Tani would reply. She too was the wife of an army man, had as many children as Mother, and struck them just as often. It took strength of character to contradict my mother but Mrs. Tani had it.

"I think it's cruel too, but since he's got so big if I spank him with my hand the only thing that hurts is my own hand!"

Mrs. Tani looked at me as if to say "Even so, it's cruel," and then went right ahead and sympathized with Mother. After that the conversation would pass to the general subject of the naughtiness of all children.

I felt rather proud when my mother said, "He's stupid." I thought to myself, That broom doesn't hurt so much. Am I the sort of guy who'd run away from a beating with that?

My father never scolded. My mother often reproached him for it, saying impatiently, "That's why the child never listens to me." On Sunday, the day that my father was usually home, she would insist that he give me a talking to.

"But today's Sunday. I'll give him a good scolding tomorrow. Hmm, s'that so? . . . Started a fight again? . . . What, he did win, did he? Hmm, that's fine. Good work, good work . . ." The more Mother nagged him about it the less concerned he seemed.

My mother was very hard to please about food; she was particularly fussy about the rice. Every time she found fault with the rice I would echo her complaints: "Yeah, it's undercooked!" But my father would say, "People with bad temperaments always find their rice is wrong.

Now, your father's rice is delicious." Wondering if it was true, I once ate some of the rice from his bowl. Of course, it was undercooked too. That's how my father avoided criticizing even the cook. He left both house and children entirely in my mother's hands. Not only did he refuse to scold, he completely refused to intervene in any household matters. He went to his unit early every morning. After he came home in the evening he usually went to his own room to read or write. So we were rarely together with him except at breakfast and dinner.

Nevertheless he did not neglect my military training. It was before he went overseas in the Sino-Japanese War, I remember, so I was still only nine or ten. Every morning he and some other officers practiced with pistols at the target range across the street from our house, and he always took me with him. He also showed me how the pistol worked and even let me shoot it. The memories I have of him riding on his horse also date from about this time. After he came home from the war he took me to another place about three miles away, called Taihōji. Live ammunition was used and there was a trench in front of the targets. He took me along with him to sit in the trench as bullets whizzed about our ears.

When I was about fourteen I took lessons in the art of fencing. Whenever the man from the swordsmith's shop brought swords to our house I butted into the conversation. Finally I was given a cheap sword of my own and was allowed to try it out; with great glee I slashed away at the straw and bamboo dummy. After I entered military cadet school, my father said that he would take me along on a cartography field trip to Sado Island during my summer vacation. But he was busy and nothing ever came of it. Once or twice I was taken along to nearby villages for a night or two to watch maneuvers. With the exception of those occasions and his teaching me some German before I went away to school, I can hardly remember any intimate conversation with my father when I was a child.

Just before the Sino-Japanese War we had a house in Katata-machi adjacent to the parade grounds. This was our fourth house in Shibata. It has since burned down. While we lived there the drill field was my playground. Between the target range and the barrack moats was an obstacle course where the troops ran races. In an area of about two or three hundred meters they had placed wooden barricades, trenches, log bridges, stone walls, and clumps of shrubbery. Everyday I went out and jumped the shrubbery, hurdled the trenches, and scrambled like a monkey over the bridges. When the troops ran the course I ran alongside, usually in the lead. Then, after the troops returned to the barricades or I tired of the game, I would go to the target range to dig for bullets.

The bullets used at the Taihōji were cylindrical but the big ones used here were round balls and quite large since they were from old-style single-shot guns. I would collect forty or fifty and, after melting them down, play at making all sorts of shapes from them. There was some risk in digging for them since the sentinel sometimes came around and often soldiers passed by. Usually I went at night when it was dark. A gang of boys saw me once and followed my example. Probably because they thought that if they were caught it would not go so badly for them if I were along, they always invited me to go with them. After joining this gang, which was made up of boys from the slum district on the outskirts of town, I made a surprising discovery. They pooled all the bullets they found and then drew lots. The loser took the bullets and sold them. They used the money to buy candy. Once I too put in the bullets I had found but managed to get out of drawing lots. After a while I fell out with the gang over something or another.

In back of the Katata-machi house was a large grove of bamboo and a number of fruit and nut trees, including plums, pears, persimmons, and chestnuts. Besides the *mōsō* variety of bamboo,[10] there was a slender bamboo that had sprouts from which we could make toy whistles. On at least one occasion, when I had an urge to see Mitsuko, I took her some of these sprouts as a gift. Such tender affairs, however, were not the only ones in which bamboo played a role.

Shibata was actually divided into two sections: Shibata-machi and Shibata-honmura. Shibata-machi had been the merchants' town while the samurai had their mansions in Shibata-honmura. It was generally so

10. *Mōsōchiku* (Phyllostachys pubescens) is a tall thick variety of bamboo often used for poles.

at that time and remains so even now. The two sections had separate schools and great differences in character and custom existed. When the children from town came to play at the parade grounds we teased them, making fun of them because they couldn't run the obstacle course or do other things as well as we could. This continued until a quarrel developed, one that took a long time to settle. On our side we had about twenty boys, most about twelve years old. I was the youngest, at only ten years old at the time, and the only officer's son. The rest were all local children. On the town side were between twenty and thirty boys. Most were around twelve but there were also three or four who were fourteen years old or older. Our battles took place on Take Street, which ran through the Naka-machi district between the town and Katata-machi. It had been tacitly agreed on as the battlefield because it was a comparatively wide street with few houses along it. The attack always came from their side and we would defend the entrance to the street.

Before the first battle I cut poles of a suitable size from the bamboo grove and handed them out to everyone on my side. The enemy came empty-handed that first time and we beat them with those poles. The next time they also carried poles. But most of theirs had been used to dry clothes on or were snatched from old fences. As soon as we came to close quarters and exchanged a few ringing blows, their weapons shattered.

I was at the very front of our side during both battles. On the other side, too, the same fellow led both times. He was a shop boy in a bean-curd store in Shimo-machi, the next district over from Naka-machi. He had a large bald spot on his head and tied his hair in a topknot to try to hide it. Though already fifteen or sixteen years old, he was still crazy about fights—the kind of person who would pay money to get into one. In fact, I heard that he had paid some coins to be allowed to join their side in this one. Looking at him always made me sick. I hated him and was determined to fix him somehow or other.

The third battle was a rock fight. Each of us had filled the front of his shirt with stones and as we advanced from a distance each side hurled them at the other. The enemy began to run out of ammunition before we did and gradually fell back. In the lead, I steadily closed on them. Soon they were completely routed—all except the fellow with the top-knot, who alone stood his ground. We grabbed him, gave him a good beating, and tossed him into a ditch. Finished with him, we withdrew in triumph.

IV.

During this time when I was so absorbed with fighting, an increasingly cruel and savage disposition seemed to develop in me. Often I would catch a harmless cat or dog and slowly beat it to death. One day on the obstacle course I killed a cat. I don't recall clearly but I think I was especially brutal—in any case, I did beat it to death. After I returned home I felt vaguely uneasy and went to bed without eating much supper. Not knowing what the trouble might be, my mother began to worry and came to stay in my bedroom. I had quite a fever and in the middle of the night suddenly bolted straight up. This so startled my mother that for the rest of the night she never took her eyes off me. Afterward she told me that I had uttered a cry amazingly like a cat. It was then, she said, that she immediately understood the whole thing. She often described it to others: "It was really horrible. Never in my whole life have I heard of anything like it. I thought how terrible it was for him being overcome by a cat's spirit! And I slapped his face and shouted at the top of my voice: 'Stupid!' Still he kept meowing and his eyes shone as big as saucers. I couldn't stand it, so I shouted again, 'How can you be such a coward and so weak after killing all those cats? Stupid!' And I slapped his face with all my might. Then he turned over on his side and went sound asleep. Really, I've never been so worried."

After that I stopped killing cats and dogs.

On another occasion at the same house in Katata-machi, a large group of junior officers came to call at New Year's. My father joined them for a while but soon retired into his own room and fell asleep. My father couldn't drink; whenever he had even a little he fell asleep. The officers, however, remained drinking in the sitting room for quite a while. Then someone shouted, "The adjutant's gone off somewhere!"

"Outrageous! Where did he run off to?" Four or five master sergeants, all dead drunk, stood up and drew their long swords. "Drag him back in here!" "We'll beat him to death if he doesn't come back!"

I was in the next room with my mother and the maid. Wondering what was happening, we listened, our hearts beating wildly. The sergeants flung open the door between the rooms and demanded of my mother, "Mrs. Ōsugi—where is the adjutant hiding?"

I snuggled close to my mother while the maid became pale and started to tremble. My mother stood up, saying, "He's not hiding. He hasn't run off to any *inn*. Please come with me and I'll show you where he is. His *inn* is his very own room and he is sound asleep in it. Sakae, you come with us."

Taking my hand she led us straight to my father's room. There she opened the door and scolded the soldiers: "Well, gentlemen, it's just as I told you. He's asleep in here. Now go ahead and beat him up if you want."

Seeing my mother's show of spirit, I took heart and stood at her side with my small fists clenched ready to fight. I thought she would jump at any one who started into Father's room. But the sergeants were awed by her menacing look. First one and then another of those in the rear dropped out of sight. Finally they all retreated.

After that the party gradually broke up, and the next day the men came to apologize. I went to the front door with my mother. It was gratifying to see their crestfallen faces. They looked so funny that I could hardly keep from laughing.

Just after my father left to go to the front, we moved into a house in Nishi-ga-wa, which was exactly the opposite kind of neighborhood though it bordered on Katata-machi. Ours was a small house behind a tailor shop run by a man named Saitō. There my mother gave birth to a boy. My father was still in Ujina waiting for the boat to sail and he wired, "NAME HIM ISAMU."

This evened the number of boys and girls in our family at three each. My third sister had been born in Katata-machi. I was now the eldest brother of six children. The eight of us, including Mother and the maid, crowded our possessions into the new house. It had only three rooms downstairs and one upstairs. There was not even a garden. In Katata-machi we had had a house with seven or eight rooms. Now we lived as frugally as possible and began to save our money.

My mother could not write any Chinese characters, only the phonetic symbols; so she had me address all her letters. Except for those to Father or Aunt Yamada, she usually had me write the letters also. She would dictate and I would rephrase her words in epistolary style. I had trouble, however, with things we hadn't yet studied at school. Mother was always very impatient but was greatly pleased when I did finish a letter and would show it to people with pride. I myself took more pride in being able to read her the mail from other people.

One day I came home from school and on entering the house called out as usual, "I'm home." Immediately I was startled: there in the room were three persons sitting with my mother—the wife of my father's groom, the maid, and a man I didn't know. A long letter was spread out before them and they all were weeping. Thinking that surely something had happened to my father, I flew to Mother's knee almost in tears myself.

"A letter has come from your father." She held me tightly, tears falling from her red and swollen eyes, as she told me about the letter. "He says there has been a terribly fierce battle and your father's horse was killed, hit four times by cannon fire."

It happened at Weihaiwei.[11] My father's battalion had seen two Japanese warships riding off the coast. Feeling secure, the battalion passed very close to the shoreline. Then the ships suddenly hauled down the Japanese flag and opened fire. They were the Chinese warships *Chen Yuan* and *Ting Yuan*. Shocked, the battalion wheeled around and fled. But on the hills in the path of their flight were other Japanese troops. These began to shoot at Father's battalion, probably thinking that the

11. From mid-January to mid-February 1895 Japanese troops besieged the fortifications around this Chinese port on the Gulf of Chihli near the tip of the Shantung Peninsula.

battalion was the enemy since they were being shelled by what appeared to be Japanese ships. Consequently, Father's battalion was pinned down between a heavy crossfire of friend and foe.

Father, as the battalion adjutant, immediately conferred with his commander and went to deliver a message to the troops on the hill. With his orderly at his side, he galloped off through the bursting Chinese shells and the hail of Japanese bullets. The orderly fell almost at once. Then Father's horse was shot out from under him. He had no choice but to leave the orderly behind. Borrowing the orderly's horse, he galloped on.

"He accomplished his mission all right," my mother said, "but his poor horse was hit four times in the belly and legs and it died there on the field. The horse died in place of your father."

My mother broke into tears again and the groom's wife and the maid cried with her. But when I thought how the horse had sacrificed its life for my father, I felt what an extraordinarily courageous thing that was and I just couldn't weep.

One day following my father's triumphant return home a group of officers who had been with the battalion at the front gathered at our house and were drinking. After the sake had been passed around several times, one of the officers slapped another on the shoulder and said, "Mrs. Ōsugi, at the time we were all ready to send a telegram reporting that this fellow had been killed instantaneously in battle. That's the truth. Even now he still has a huge scar. Hey, take off your shirt and show them. Come on! what are you worried about? It's an honorable wound. Isn't that so, Mrs. Ōsugi?"

They forced the man to take off his shirt. On the officer's back, which was bright red from drinking, was a huge scar. It was as if a gash had been gouged all the way from the left shoulder across to the right armpit.

"You see! And his arm is held on only by scar tissue," the man went on, holding up the other's arm so that we could see. Just as he said, the arm had a scar running almost entirely around it.

"Oh!" my mother gasped and turned her face away in spite of herself. I too felt a little queer inside.

As this officer did, my father's horse regained life after first being reported dead and was brought home lame. Father talked with my mother and said that he wanted to shoot it. But he had raised the horse himself and couldn't bring himself to such an act. He finally sold the animal.

It was at that time my father received the Imperial Order of the Golden Kite.[12]

I have written that some of the houses we lived in while in Shibata had burned down. This happened in a great fire known as the Yomo Shichi fire that occurred during Father's absence at the front.

I've forgotten the month, but I think it was after the weather turned chilly. The fire broke out one night about eleven o'clock. We were living in Nishi-ga-wa, which was almost the western limits of town, and the fire started at the other end of town. We watched the blaze for about an hour. It looked as if it was not going to be easy to put out. Growing larger and larger, the flames spread toward our neighborhood.

I immediately ran out to watch close up. For an hour I moved here and there watching the fire. At one point I went right up to the fire—or rather, it came right up to where I was standing. The tongues of the flames licked at the rooftops as they raced toward me. As I stood there looking I suddenly realized that no one was running toward the fire any more; everyone was fleeing from it. Although I intended to stay four or five hundred yards away, I had dropped my guard and the fire had come right on me. The weather had been fair for some time and the thin shingles on the roofs had become so dry that they were warped. The flames traveled along the tops of the roofs, leaping the gaps where streets intervened. Everybody was racing about. Finally even the firemen fled. I ran hard in the direction of home. After going two or three hundred yards I glanced back and saw the Kishibojin temple[13]—the spot where I had been standing—catch on fire. Its huge thatched roof burst into one great pillar of fire.

The fire was still eight hundred to a thousand yards away, but I thought it was just a matter of time before it reached our house. As soon

12. This military decoration for bravery carried with it a small life annuity.
13. Kishibojin, it might be noted, is a goddess who protects children.

as I got home I told my mother we should pack our bags. Everyone else in the neighborhood had already started to pack up.

My mother wouldn't listen, answering, "We should be ashamed to get so excited." But the fire came steadily closer and I knew it would be here within an hour. I begged her at least to get the bags ready.

"There will still be plenty of time for packing after everyone else has left. It wouldn't do to rush off only to be laughed at afterwards. Go out and take another look." Nevertheless she gave orders to the maid to get ready. After a while longer she called me back and handed me a bundle.

"It is getting more and more dangerous, so take the children and get out of the house. You know the tall ginkgo tree right in the middle of the parade grounds, don't you? Go there, all right? Don't leave there." Then she put my youngest brother on my sister's back and sent us off.

It was three or four hundred yards to the entrance of the parade grounds from Nishi-ga-wa. Already the grounds were cluttered with baggage. We took possession of the area around the tree just as Mother had told us to.

The tree was between the target range and our former house. An army man named Akiyama lived in the house now and Mother had told me, "Be sure to let Mrs. Akiyama know that you are at the ginkgo tree." The Akiyamas were not worried. Since they had a large backyard and their house was separated from the rest of the neighborhood, they were sure they would be safe whatever happened. But as I was on my way back to the ginkgo tree I saw something that looked like a huge ball of fire fall out of the sky and land on their roof. The roof burst into flames so suddenly that I jerked back.

Later my mother and the maid appeared, carrying a few things from our home. Wrapping myself in a quilt, I went to sleep. The fire raged until almost noon the next day and nearly all of Shibata-machi and part of Shibata-honmura burned—a total of some twenty-five hundred houses.

Decades before, there had been another fire called Yomo Shichi. It was named after a man who had been falsely accused of a crime, cruelly tortured, and executed. Afterward people talked of a curse. As a matter of fact, some said that the house where the Akiyamas lived had then been the home of the very official who tortured Yomo Shichi. Moreover, all the houses around there except this one survived the fire. Many people also swore that they had seen elsewhere the same kind of ball of fire I saw and that the same thing had happened to other houses. Almost all the houses had been old ones, with thatched roofs, like the Akiyamas'.

Where our house was is today just a big empty lot. In the courtyard of the Suwa Shrine, where the statue of Ōkura Kihachirō stands, is another small shrine—the Yomo Shichi Shrine. It is dedicated to services for the spirit of Yomo Shichi.

CHAPTER 2

CHILDHOOD
1894-1895

I.

In the evening of the day after we were burned out of our house we moved in with an army family named Ōtachime, close friends of my parents. Their house was behind the elementary school next to the parade grounds. There were six or seven children in the family. The oldest, named Akira, was two years older and two grades ahead of me in school. He was rather stupid and I had always treated him with contempt because of it. As soon as I moved in, we started to quarrel. The next day I knocked him into the ditch in front of his house. Covered with mud and crying, he ran into the house. Before making him change his clothes, his mother slapped him a few times, saying, "What kind of a kid are you, to bawl when you're beaten by someone younger than you?"

Surprisingly, my mother hardly scolded me at all. Instead she put on her coat and went out somewhere. Early the next morning we moved in with a woman teacher from the elementary school. Her house had only three rooms, including the entrance hall; we borrowed the use of the small six-mat[1] living room while the teacher lived alone in the next room.

1. A standard single tatami mat is roughly three feet by six feet, so the room was about nine feet by twelve.

"This is because you're always picking fights," Mother said, scowling at me a little. Still frowning, she turned to the maid, who was carrying in some luggage on her back: "It'd really do him good to lose sometimes." Then she laughed. "And next time he picks a fight it'll be with the teacher!"

After we had lived there a couple of weeks, a little house four or five doors down the street became vacant and we moved in. There was a large compound with three buildings in it; one had been divided into a two-family dwelling. A family named Yokoi, who must have been in the army, lived in one half and we lived in the other. The largest building was the home of a Major Ishikawa. Ours fronted on Hachiken-chō with its back to the other two and was set apart by a fence. In the house next door was a family named Yamagata, whose father was either a captain or a major in the army. My own father had just been promoted to captain on the battlefield.

There were four or five Yamagata boys; the eldest, Tarō, was two or three years older than I. He attended the Aizu Middle School and was away at school most of the time. The next eldest, Jirō, was a very good friend of mine. Major Ishikawa had two sons, the older about the same age as Tarō. In the Yokoi family there was one boy, who was my age. Except for this boy, Yellow Jaundice as we called him, I had no enemies. And except for my teasing him, he wasn't really an enemy. All of us, including the son of a Captain Ōkubo who lived diagonally across the street from the Ishikawas, immediately became friends. Yet there wasn't much close friendship among us. We never fought among ourselves but we held one another in mutual contempt. Ishikawa and Ōkubo had lived across the street from one another for a long time and were on good terms. I couldn't stomach either of these two refined "young gentlemen" and they made fun of me for being rustic. The Yamagatas' Jirō was also a young gentleman. But he had lived in town for a long time and attended the town elementary school, so his "refinement" was of a different sort from that of Ishikawa or Ōkubo. Consequently he couldn't really be intimate with the other two. Jirō's townsman refinement disgusted me, and I detected a latent brutality hidden in him. He often amused himself by tormenting his younger brother while

I passed the time teasing Yellow Jaundice. We called Yokoi that because of the yellow cast to his face. He did look undernourished. He and his younger sister, who had the same thin yellow face, played forlornly together.

Although our mothers were all the wives of officers, they had almost nothing to do with one another.

A ghost appeared at the Yamagata house. In the middle of the night a match was heard being struck in the kitchen. There was the sound of a fire burning in the stove, of something being cut on top of the chopping board; there were footsteps; a cupboard squeaked as it was opened; teacups rattled. And there was the sound of a voice. This disturbance continued for a full hour one night.

Another night, when Mrs. Yamagata was returning from a trip to the toilet, she opened the outside door intending to wash her hands. A large full moon hung suspended between the pine trees in the garden and it was as bright as day outside. Reaching for the pot of water, she could see the moon reflected on the surface of the water. Then, as she started to scoop up some water, big drops of rain suddenly began to fall. Thinking it strange, she raised her head and looked—the full moon was shining brightly among the pines without a sign of rain. Again she bent over the pot of water. Again, as she did so, rain started to fall. Frightened, she fled back to her bedroom.

Late the following night Mrs. Yamagata woke up again. She started toward the toilet but, opening the sliding door, heard something heavy fall with a bang at her feet and then roll away. Peering into the darkness after the sound of the rolling object, she had a queer feeling of uneasiness. Then the huge head of a man appeared in sharp outline against the pitch black. Mrs. Yamagata uttered a little cry and collapsed.

The next time, two or three nights later, she saw a huge figure standing on the veranda. After that, the Yamagata household fell into chaos. Four or five young men from town and around the neighborhood came to stay in the house. They kept oak clubs at their sides and stayed up all night drinking. Although the ghost did not show up for the next few nights, as soon as the youths left it appeared again. This same thing happened over and over again until Mrs. Yamagata called in a priest, one in whom she had great faith, to say prayers. He stayed for some days. I don't quite remember now whether the ghost did disappear under the influence of the prayers but the priest seems to have been of questionable character.

The Ishikawas and the Ōkubos took no part in the talk about the ghost. Yet it was rumored that they had some sort of plan in case it became necessary to have the priest stay with them. As for Mrs. Yamagata, she was a rather saucy sort.

At about that time the Women's League held a meeting to pray for victory in the war and the safety of all their husbands. The same priest who was involved in the other matter showed up at the ceremony; there was some story about somebody's wife clinging to his side. Moreover, this priest's temple was in Sutani Valley in the mountains about eight miles from Shibata, and there was also talk about some wives who went clear out there on pilgrimages.

The ghost appeared at our house just once. Mother was sick and had gone to a hot springs somewhere. During her absence my younger sister and the maid awoke suddenly in the middle of the night. While they were lying there trying to get back to sleep, the same clatter started in the kitchen. Trembling, they listened in silence. Just then the Yokois' small house dog began to bark. A few minutes later the ghost fled. The younger children and I, who were lying in the next room, all slept through the whole thing.

The next day when I was told about this, I said it was stupid and laughed at them. Nevertheless the maid, worried and frightened, sent Mother a telegram calling her home immediately. Mother comforted us all: "As long as your mother and elder brother are here, you're safe." She didn't really look the least bit worried.

Yamagata Tarō entered the military cadet school in Nagoya two years ahead of me. Four or five years later when I met him there, he said that he had heard the noises with his own ears and believed in the ghost.

It appeared once more, this time at the home of a soldier who was killed in the war. In the middle of the night his young wife had the feeling that her name was being called and opened her eyes. Standing at the head of her bed was her husband, covered with blood. The next morning she received the telegram informing her that her husband had died honorably in battle.

II.

After we had lived in the Hachiken-chō house for two or three months, we moved to a place on the next block, Niken-chō, directly across from the upper elementary school. It was there, toward the end of my tenth year, that I first awakened to the pleasures of sex.

An army family named Kawamura had also been burned out in the fires and the wife rented a place in the neighborhood. My mother and Mrs. Kawamura were as close as two sisters. I also liked Mrs. Kawamura very much and her daughter, Ohana, even more. Ohana was the same age as I or a little younger. She came to our house almost every day and usually played just with me rather than with my sisters. When all of us were together, we often played cards in the *kotatsu* with a blanket spread over the low table to keep our legs and feet warm.[2] At those times Ohana always sat next to me. Then our hands would meet under the blanket and clasp tightly or just our fingertips would suddenly touch. We both enjoyed the contact, which led to real [sex play][3] before we knew it.

Neither Ohana nor I was satisfied with just this. So frequently we would go up to my room on the second floor and spend several hours together. There we could play at being adults without anyone else interfering.

Another girl who was my friend was the daughter of an army family named Senda who lived in the same neighborhood. I've forgotten what it was I had done wrong but one day my mother insisted I apologize. The more insistent she became the more I felt I couldn't apologize. After

2. A *kotatsu* is a space several feet square created below the level of the mat floor to accommodate the legs and usually, as here, furnished with quilts and perhaps with a heat source for use in cold weather.

3. In this first example of a number of passages to do with sexuality or politics that were censored in the prewar edition, the only deletion here was *sei* (sex)—two-thirds of the word *asobi* (to play or amuse); readers would have needed little sophistication to fill in the blanks.

dinner Mother said, "I can't put up with such a stubborn child any more. We're going to Aunt Yamada's in Tokyo." She had the maid and the children change their clothes, and then she took them all and left carrying a small wicker suitcase. I thought she didn't mean it when she said they were going to Tokyo, but she made such elaborate preparations that I wondered if they weren't really going somewhere. I thought to myself that maybe I should have apologized.

Two or three hours later I heard a lot of noise at the front door. They were all returning. With them were Mrs. Senda and her daughter, Reichan. Mrs. Senda came to my bedroom and begged me, "Auntie will apologize for you. Say you won't ever do it again, all right?" But I thought that she and my mother had talked it all over beforehand, so I no longer wanted to apologize.

"Look for yourself. They've all come back, haven't they?" I did agree with her but pulled the covers over my head and said nothing. I heard my mother state, "I told you how stubborn he was, didn't I?" The two of them seemed to be discussing ways of dealing with me. Mrs. Senda reproached my mother, saying "You mustn't go too far," and urged her to drop the matter and go to bed.

Meanwhile Reichan came to my bedside and, stealing her hand under the covers, grasped my hand: "Sakae, I'll apologize for you, so it'll be all right. You won't do it again so you'll be forgiven, okay? I'll say you're sorry for you, okay? I'll apologize for you." She pulled the covers back and looked at my face, repeating over and over, "Okay? okay?" The tight feeling in my chest gradually faded and I finally nodded in silence.

Ohana attended the elementary school in town, so I never saw her in school. But Reichan went to my school in the grade below mine, while Mitsuko was in my class. Reichan had a reputation as the prettiest girl in her class and was the best student too. Mitsuko was the best student in our class, but when it came to looks she had a strong rival named Kinukawa Tamako.

Tamako was the daughter of a retired army man. She was quite cute with her round face, plump cheeks, and large eyes. But I couldn't stomach the air of self-conceit about her. She always wore pretty clothes and would strut with self-assurance as she passed by on her frequent social calls. Even now when I think of her I think of a little princess.

Mitsuko was the daughter of a low-ranking pharmacist or some such person at the garrison hospital. Her clothes were always dirty. Her eyes were narrow and the complexion of her thin, hollow-cheeked face was very poor with a reddish coarseness to it—not at all like the rosy color of Tamako's.

One day I lay in wait for Tamako and blocked her path. Puffing out her cheeks, she merely stared at me. I hated this kind of attitude. Mitsuko would have shouted, "Stop it!" or something similar, pushed me aside, and gone on her way. Since that is what I expected, I often blocked Mitsuko's path.

Ishikawa and Ōkubo, who were both quite handsome, were admirers of Tamako. This made me dislike her even more, so I became an admirer of Mitsuko.

Next door to our house in Niken-chō lived a family named Yoshida who, by local standards, were wealthy. I became friends with their son who was just about my age. Soon, however, I stopped playing with the boy in favor of his mother.

Mrs. Yoshida had cut her hair short after a shower of sparks fell on it during the fire. Above one eyebrow she had a large mole that looked like a wart. She was not a very attractive woman. She often tutored her son and me in English and arithmetic. When she praised me for learning well, she had the habit of hugging me tightly, her cheek pressed against mine, as a reward. These rewards made me very happy. Once when her son was out of the room and the mother was rewarding me in this way, she said, "I didn't come to this house as a bride. I was tricked into it. And soon I'm going to leave here." Afterward I heard that she actually did leave.

Behind that house was a large rice field. One night there was a drizzling rain and far off on the other side of the field I saw what is called a "fox's marriage." Three or four lights—like paper lanterns—appeared

and then disappeared, only to reappear somewhere else. As I was thinking I had never seen anything like that, suddenly a line hundreds of
meters long lit up all at once. Then it too disappeared. Wondering if I
could be imagining it, I watched as it appeared again. This time it spread
until the distant field became a solid sheet of twinkling lights.

Mrs. Yoshida said, "It's only caused by the sulphur," and one night
she brought out some wax matches of a type I had never seen before.
She used one to draw a man's face on a rain-soaked fence. The outline
of a pale ghostlike face appeared, glowing dimly. Half afraid and half
fascinated, I did what she told me and slowly touched it with my finger.
My fingertip gave off a pale glow. I rubbed my finger around the ghost's
face; the places I touched all began to glow. "You're not the least bit
afraid, are you?" she said, hugging me and pressing her cheek to mine
until she made my face glow too.

Later I heard a legend about the fox's marriage. Once upon a time
two lords fought at this place. One was the attacker and the other the
defender. The defending lord knew that he was no match for the other,
so he devised a strategy. The area was covered with swampy land that
appeared at first glance to be merely pools of water but were actually
seas of mud so deep that anyone who fell in immediately sank from
sight. The lord ordered his troops to entice the unwary enemy into these
bogs. They put on footwear ordinarily used for walking on snow and
ran across the swamps pretending to be in full retreat. The enemy pur-
sued them, plunged into the mud, and sank out of sight. The will-o'-
the-wisps I saw were their departed spirits coming back to haunt. As a
matter of fact, when I lived there one still found human bones, spears,
swords, armor, and the like in the vicinity.

III.

Shortly before my father returned from the war we moved into yet another house in Katata-machi, four or five doors away from our former
place. While living there I attended two years of upper elementary
school. I had always done well in school, never lower than third in my
class from the first grade of primary through the second year of upper

elementary school.[4] In the upper elementary school, however, I could never stay ahead of a boy named Ōsawa, who had gone through the primary grades in the town school. He stayed at the head of the class both years, while Ōkubo or I came in second. Ōkubo was one year older than I and Ōsawa was two years older.

While in upper elementary school I also studied English, mathematics, and classical Chinese with private tutors. My English tutor was named Hayami and lived next door to our former house in Katata-machi. I don't know what sort of education he had but he was very stylish and gave the appearance of being very much the rake. His students came from morning to night and there were almost always thirty or forty in attendance.

I think I started classical Chinese and mathematics after the English tutor left, but I've completely forgotten the name of the first of these teachers or even what he looked like. I recall only that his house was in Soto-ga-wa behind the army barracks. My second Chinese tutor was a warder at the local prison. He was short with a pale face and quite shabby appearance. His house was shabby as well. Since he left for work early, it was always still dark when I went to his house for my morning lesson. Along with me he had two or three other pupils.

In the winter the snow was three or four feet deep and I would almost freeze as I made my way to the tutor's house through the drifts that were not yet packed down. As soon as I arrived, his mother, looking extremely cold, would come and put a little charcoal dust in the small brazier. By blowing very hard she would finally get a fire started. I felt very sorry for her and told my mother about it. She immediately had my father's groom take two bushels of charcoal to the woman, who cried as she thanked him and from that day on always made me a roaring fire with large chunks.

4. In the 1890s public elementary schooling was divided into the first four primary grades (*jinjō shōgakkō*), which were compulsory, and the next two years (kōtō shōgakkō), which—because of funding difficulties—were not made mandatory until 1907. The more important break came at the next level, the lower secondary or middle school (*chūgakkō*), which was for the more ambitious who could afford the costs. The beginning of middle school also marked the end of coeducational schooling. Most higher secondary schools (*kōtōgakkō*) for males were strictly college preparatory.

I finished reading the Four Books—*The Confucian Analects, The Book of Mencius, The Doctrine of the Mean,* and *The Great Learning*—under this teacher. He was about twenty-five—or at the oldest, twenty-seven or twenty-eight—and didn't cut a very impressive figure. His mother's clothes were always dirty but her face had a refined quality. It was not in the least unusual for me to see samurai families who had come down in the world in such fashion. Since that time I have been a prisoner in jail several times and each time I have thought of that teacher. He was very quiet and rather shy, even when he scolded his pupils. He must have had a desk job in the jail that didn't require him to deal directly with the prisoners. He wasn't the type of teacher who could speak roughly or scold a prisoner.

About that time, four or five friends began to gather at my house and we started a small club in which we read essays, gave lectures, and wrote compositions. The other regular members were Nishimura Torakō, who lived one house away; Sugiura, from town; and Tani, whose mother I've already talked about.[5] Torakō and Sugiura were in the grade ahead of me. Both were tutored by Professor Shibayama in the neighborhood and so Torakō brought Sugiura along to our club. Tani was a year younger than I.

I read a great deal and always took the lead in the group. Among all my friends I was almost the first to read the magazine *World of Young People*.[6] Then I discovered a wonderful bookstore and purchased all kinds of books to read. Furthermore, I owned a collection of moral anecdotes in translation as well as four or five large volumes of essays that none of the others knew about. The lectures and essays that I secretly took from these or from the magazines never failed to win their praises.

The bookstore named Nakamura's Banshōdō was in the town of Suibara, seven or eight miles southwest of Shibata. One of the clerks or

5. There is some confusion in the 1930 Kaizō edition; it gives the name as Ōtani, in apparent reference to Mrs. Tani, the friend of Ōsugi's mother mentioned in chapter 1 part 3.

6. *Shōnen sekai* was published twice a month by the Hakubunkan in Tokyo. In addition to articles and other features, it printed essays by its readers. For analysis of the motifs in youth magazines of the day, see Earl H. Kinmonth, *The Self-Made Man in Meiji Japanese Thought.*

shop boys had come to Shibata and was living in a tenement off a back alley. I found out about him somehow and became probably his first customer when I went to buy some book or other. He had no store or anything like one—just a few dozen books lined up in one corner of his living room. But in a town like Shibata where only one variety store served both as a stationery and textbook shop, his volumes were enough to seem like a tremendous selection. Whenever I had free time, I used to visit the place and read lying down. Although I received no allowance, when I needed books or stationery I could charge them without even asking my mother first. If I ran up too large a bill, she might warn me to ask beforehand but never scolded me for it.

Soon afterward, the man moved into a store in Kamimachi and named it the Banshōdō. Until I left Shibata three or four years later I was that store's best customer. Last summer, when I made the trip back to Shibata, the first thing I did—partly because my inn was close by—was to visit that bookstore. The same man still ran it.

"Do you recognize me?" I asked him as he stared at me in silence.

"I certainly recall the face all right, but I can't recall where."

"Well, it has been all of twenty years. I don't blame you for not remembering."

"No, wait. Now I recall the voice. It certainly has been a long time, hasn't it." He had the shop boy bring us some tea and then I listened to him tell all about the whereabouts of my old friends. The shopkeeper had graduated from Shibata Middle School, so he knew practically all of them.

In telling the story of the bookstore I've digressed from the subject of my friends and our club. Let me return to it for a bit. The club's greatest topic was the return of the Liaotung Peninsula. I found a contribution in the readers' section in *World of Young People* entitled "On Vengeance" and delivered it as a lecture.[7] Almost in tears, everyone there

7. Defeated in the Sino-Japanese War, China signed the April 1895 Treaty of Shimonoseki, ceding part of the Liaotung Peninsula to Japan. Within the week, however, Russia, Germany, and France intervened to block Japan from taking possession. This "retrocession" of the peninsula forced upon the Japanese caused a public outcry against the "triple intervention" and is mentioned several times in the following chapters.

swore revenge. I urged them to memorize the Imperial Rescript on the Retrocession of the Liaotung Peninsula and I recited the whole thing in a loud voice every morning as soon as I arose.

Torakō moved to Hokkaido as a clerk right after he graduated from upper elementary school. There hasn't been any news of him in fifteen or twenty years. Tani entered military cadet school one year after I did and is probably a major by now. I don't know what Sugiura's father did for a living but, judging from his terrible stinginess despite the nice house he lived in, I suppose that he must have been a moneylender. When I was back in Shibata I asked about Sugiura and heard that the family became the town's biggest landowner and Sugiura now just lounges about as head of the family.

When I visited him he explained at length about his relations with the farmers. "I don't know about other places, but at least one can say about Shibata that there aren't any farmer movements going to start up around here. And you know, that's because rather than a relation of lord and vassal, it's one of parent and children—and the landlords here take good care of their tenants." As he talked, he moved about the room using his fan with grace to carefully extinguish the candles in the household altars.

IV.

Thus, in those days I studied hard but also played hard. My playground had changed since I lived in Katata-machi. I no longer went to the parade grounds. Now I hunted grasshoppers at the target range in Taihōji, searched for mushrooms in the hills behind it, and caught crabs in the marshes around Ijiminoyama, the amusement grounds of ancient lords. I also wandered around the clear streams at Kajiyama and climbed above the ruins of the castle where three hundred years earlier some lord, his castle besieged and his water supply cut off by the enemy, had

---

The essay's actual title, "Gashin shōtan ron," referred to the slogan used by the Japanese government to counter public criticism of its handling of the affair and alluded to a prince in ancient China who was said to keep a container of gall by his side the better to nurse his vengeance against victorious enemies.

taken rice from his storehouse and poured it over the backs of his horses in order to fool his opponent. If you dug a bit in the red clay of the small plain at the top of the mountain, you could still find the rice charred black by fire.

All these places were within two or three miles of my house and perfect for our hikes. One summer day when Torakō and I went to play at Kajiyama, we found the mountain lilies in full bloom. Torakō began to dig for bulbs. Because his house had a large garden in back and he often helped his elderly grandmother with her plants, he knew a great deal about such things. I too started to dig. We had a good harvest; thinking, Torakō's family is poor, I decided to give all the bulbs to him. Torakō also liked fishing. On the many occasions that we set out together at three o'clock in the morning, I always let him keep everything we caught. But as we were on the way home this day I suddenly remembered my mother, who wasn't feeling well and had stayed in bed. I got the idea of taking some flowers home for her. I ran all over gathering the biggest lilies with the most blooms I could find. The two of us returned home elated. As soon as I got to the house I went to where Mother was sleeping.

Barely glancing at the flowers, which were already wilting, Mother said, "You should have brought the bulbs home. You are really stupid!" She criticized me for giving away the lily bulbs: "And you're always so concerned about Torakō."

I've never been so sad. I didn't cry but felt as if I were all tied up inside. Dejected, I went to my own room without being able to say anything in my own defense—or rather without even feeling like trying to explain. I know that if I had just told her why, she would have apologized and praised me; yet this is the saddest memory I have of my mother.

Nonetheless I loved my mother. One evening that same summer our family was enjoying the coolness of the living room when suddenly my sister, gazing out into the garden, gave a shriek. Startled, we turned to look out at the garden. There in one corner was something with one huge, glittering eye. Frightened, all that we children could say was

"Oh!" But Mother stood up, slipped on a pair of clogs, and went out into the garden. We watched without speaking.

"Come here, all of you! There's nothing to be afraid of," she called. "Here is your real ghost," she said, showing us what we had thought so frightening. It was a tin can lying on its side.

Nevertheless, probably because I became harder to deal with as I grew older, Mother's punishments came to be increasingly harsh. I remember an occasion when she and the maid tied me up with a rope and both of them beat me severely because I hadn't minded the maid while Mother was out. My mother often left the children for half the day or more while she visited neighborhood friends, mostly other army wives. The maid had complete authority at such times.

I also got into a lot of fights. My mother would often grumble about all the complaints my fighting caused, saying, "I've never had to apologize for anything I have done; yet all I do is apologize for something this kid has done." Again and again I would do something bad that my parents would have to apologize for.

One day during my second year in upper elementary school I had a quarrel with a fellow named Nishikawa. He was in the same grade but in a different class. I was the toughest boy in my class and he was the toughest in his. Thinking that my usual route home would be dangerous that day, I selected a thin piece of metal—a rod used as a paperweight on our writing pad—and slipped it into my shirt front. Then I set out from school trying to look nonchalant. Nishikawa followed me just as I expected. Seven or eight of his friends trailed along behind him. I took the usual way home and entered the parade grounds next to the garrison hospital. As soon as I was inside the grounds I stuck my right hand in my shirt and got ready. Up until then the others had stayed their distance. Now they drew closer, making a lot of noise. They cursed me and dared me to fight. Suddenly someone ran up behind me and a voice yelled, "Come on! Fight!" Grasping the metal rod, I wheeled around. Nishikawa had his fist raised to hit me. Without warning I struck out with the rod. Nishikawa half turned and blood gushed from his head. Everyone was shocked and gathered around him. I withdrew feeling triumphant as well as a little worried. From that day on Nishikawa had a two-inch spot on his head where no hair would grow.

One day, a long time after that incident, my father returned home from the regiment and immediately called me into his room. He and my mother faced me, both with very worried expressions. "Is it true you hit or kicked someone in the head at school the other day?" Father asked sternly, looking quite upset. I could see the veins in his forehead swelling. This was the first time that my father had ever put me on trial this way and I could sense that something important was involved. Yet I couldn't recall hitting anyone recently. Then my mother spoke, asking me if I knew a certain boy.

I did know him since we were in the same class. He wasn't a close friend, but I knew him from school. Increasingly puzzled as to what this was all about, I answered only that I did know him.

Mother, who had been waiting for my answer, then asked, "Didn't you kick or hit him in the back of the neck?"

Now even more mystified since I could not recall anything of the sort, I answered, "No."

Finally Mother relaxed and told me the whole story. Major Okada, the regimental commander, lived in Hachiken-chō. My father was his adjutant. According to Major Okada, his groom or orderly was cleaning up in front of the house when a schoolboy passed. The boy was staggering from one side of the street to the other and several times fell down in the gutter in front of the house. Puzzled, the man took the boy by the arm and questioned him.

"They say he told them you had done it," my mother said. "Anyway, they took him to his home. The doctor said that he had been struck at a spot on the base of the skull so vulnerable that you can kill a man by just sticking him there with a needle. Even if he recovers, he will probably be an idiot the rest of his life."

Then I remembered. Every rainy day at school we used to play a game called Capture-the-Corner. Each side stationed itself in part of the gym we used for exercise. Then one side would try to force the other defenders out of the way and occupy their camp. Sometimes, however, the game couldn't be decided just by pushing and shoving according to the rules. So when the first assault had done its damage and the enemy lines were beginning to crumble, one or two volunteers would leap into the gap. They would climb on someone's shoulders and jump over the others deep into the enemy's territory, thus occupying their camp at one fell swoop. This volunteer mission was my specialty. I wondered if I might not have kicked someone in the neck when I was leaping over his head.

I told my parents about the game and the three of us decided that events must have happened that way. My father immediately went to pay a sick call on the boy. The family deeply appreciated the call and nothing more came of the matter. I don't remember exactly what became of the boy, but I think he had a slight squint afterward and never spoke much.

A YOUNG
HOOLIGAN
1895-1899

I.

One day shortly before the end of my second year in upper elementary school,[1] our teacher told Ōsawa, Ōkubo, and me to come to his lodgings that night. The three of us were quite worried. It was the first time that a teacher had ever told any of us to come to his home. Though we put our heads together we couldn't guess what the matter could be. This made us even more nervous. We met beforehand and together timidly walked to the teacher's place in Jizōdō.

The teacher met us with a smile; he himself poured us tea. He told us to relax and sit cross-legged instead of in formal fashion. Then, his white teeth shining in his very dark face, he broached the subject. "We're going to get a middle school in this area soon. How about you three seeing if you could go?"

We were vaguely aware of rumors about a middle school, but we hadn't felt concerned since they weren't definite and we didn't know if students would be allowed to enter right after finishing two years of

---

1. The original chapter title was *furyōshōnen*, which might be rendered more simply as "bad boy" or, somewhat more anachronistically, "juvenile delinquent." On the public school system at this time, see chapter 2 note 4.

upper elementary school. Not knowing what to say, the three of us just looked at one another for a while without speaking.

"You can enter as soon as you finish your second year of upper elementary school, you know. Moreover, I will sponsor the three of you, so why don't you try it? Go home and tell your fathers and mothers that your teacher told you this and discuss it with them."

We were as elated as if we were already enrolled in middle school. We went home overjoyed, hardly paying attention to the teacher's warning: "But don't tell anyone else about this, all right?"

The teacher was young and probably fresh out of normal school. Except for the fourth-grade teacher named Shima, all our teachers had been rather old. He was the first teacher to ever really become our friend and join in students' games. He was also the only teacher to use informal language in speaking to us. Immediately on his arrival in Shibata, he took charge of our first-year class. When first we met him we didn't care for his swarthy face. It frightened us a little.

Our first impression was changed, however, as soon as we saw him in singing class. He was in charge of it also, though in the past singing class had always been led by a woman teacher. This in itself gave him a certain novelty and popularity. For a while we considered him a real curiosity. Sitting there in front of the organ with his dark face, he held his body erect and his chest stuck out like a soldier's. We waited eagerly to hear what sort of sound was going to come from that organ. It wasn't particularly different from the sound produced by the women teachers with their gentle faces. Yet, despite the dark face and disheveled hair, his large fingers raced across the keys with a liveliness and skill that were not at all clumsy, and his playing gave us a feeling of exhilaration. Then he began to sing. His wide mouth filled his whole dark face and from it came a deep bass that reverberated throughout the classroom. Up to then we had heard only women teachers sing, their lips pursed and voices barely audible. Now under his influence we became exuberant, opened our mouths as wide as possible, and sang as loudly as we could.

There is something else that I should write in capital letters: he was the only teacher from whom I never once received a scolding. Even so, for some reason I have completely forgotten the name of this man who was so good to me for two years.

Although the teacher had strictly forbidden us to talk about his recommending us to middle school, we told everyone. We also spread the word that the plans for the middle school were definite and that one could enter after two years of upper elementary school. Many others from our class wanted to be admitted and consequently we three became the objects of resentment.

At the beginning of April I took my admission application to the temple that served as the temporary building for the middle school. The official in charge read it through and then thrust it back at me: "You're not old enough. We can't."

I returned home almost in tears. According to the entrance regulations you had to be twelve or older. According to my papers I was eleven years and eleven months—one month shy. I could hardly contain my chagrin. Father and Mother both tried to console me, saying, "There's no need to be in such a hurry. Next year will be all right." But I just couldn't stop thinking about it. I could see everyone laughing at me and saying, "Serves him right!"

I corrected the record of my age from eleven years eleven months to eleven years twelve months and went to try again at the school office.

"It isn't really eleven months—it's twelve months, you see! And if it's twelve months then it makes a total of twelve years, so it's all right, isn't it?" As if my life depended on it, I counted on my fingers from May— the month I was born in—through April and argued emphatically that it came to twelve months.

The school official laughed but took my application, saying, "Well, we'll discuss it and see." The next day I went back again. In the end I was allowed to enter because everyone was to be admitted for one term on probation and students would not become permanent until September.

Beside Ōsawa, Ōkubo, and me, about twenty from our class enrolled in the middle school that spring. About half of them were rejected when

it came time for permanent admissions; the majority of the other half
failed by the end of the first year. The remaining one or two failed to
advance into the third year.

II.

It was during the summer of my thirteenth year that a great change came
over me both physically and mentally. One day I suddenly discovered
thick black hairs on parts of my body where not even down had been
growing. I was extremely embarrassed, for I had never seen this even on
any friends a year or two older than I, much less on friends of the same
age. Secretly, in the toilet or in my own room, repeatedly I ———.[2]
Then more than ever, it ———.

Almost at the same time I learned about real masturbation. Before,
with Ohana, it had been merely play; now it became ———. Now I
could no longer read at my desk for any length of time. I couldn't sit for
even an hour before ——— and I could not stay still however I tried.
Two or three times a day I would turn to masturbating. I, who had been
so studious, became a complete idler.

I had never seen or even heard my parents do or say anything un-
chaste. I had, however, often seen the orderly or the groom carry on
with the maid. Since the groom lived outside our household, it was not
very frequent. But the orderly was like a male servant or houseboy and
he and the maid flirted constantly. Once I had gone into the orderly's
room for something and found them doing what he said was "wrestling." And once I had collided with the maid as she hurried from his
room; flushed and short of breath, she was fastening the front of her
kimono. Finally the maid became pregnant with his child and returned
to her home for a while.

Okohito-machi, behind Katata-machi where we lived, was a prostitution district. There was another at the end of Katata-machi next to
Nishi-ga-wa. Every Sunday evening you could see drunken soldiers

2. This is one of the few passages so heavily censored that the exact meaning is
difficult to reconstruct from the remains of a sentence or clause. The general meaning, of
course, is clear.

passing by with their arms around the women's powdered necks. The groom once took me along to a bathhouse at some "hot spring" in Nishi-ga-wa. There was a crowd of women, all with their necks powdered white. With them were two or three men. The groom told me to wait for him and went into the bathhouse alone. I could see men and women entering the large tub together, all laughing and squealing. Even though the groom had told me to wait, I became annoyed and went home by myself.

I was gradually drifting away from the girls who had been my friends. Mitsuko, whom I rarely had a chance to see since we entered separate schools, often came for a walk in the evening at the nearby parade grounds. She brought her little brother along, but there was no doubt that she really came to see me; the little brother was her excuse to get out of the house. Spotting her, I would run straight to the parade grounds and we would stop three or four yards apart. Just to exchange smiles was enough for her. She would go home satisfied.

Things never went beyond that with Mitsuko and me. I can't recall ever speaking to her—or rather, I should say that we never talked together. Yet in my mind, at least, we were great lovers. I don't know what became of her afterward. Her older sister, who was no more beautiful than Mitsuko, went to the teachers' school in Niigata. Such studies were the only chance for girls who were bright but poor and I heard that Mitsuko was destined to follow her sister.

After Mitsuko and I parted—or possibly just before that—there was another girl, who came with her smaller sister to walk at the parade grounds. She too came just to exchange smiles with me. She was the daughter of the police chief and, again, we never spoke to each other. Only once did I actually come face-to-face with her. I took a letter from my father to the police chief's official residence; when I called at the front door she appeared unexpectedly. Both of us blushed and neither could say anything. I held out the letter and she took it without a word, running quickly inside. She had full red lips. But I've forgotten where or when we first met. Our relationship never went any further; surprisingly, I can still remember her name.

Ohana and Reichan both faded from my thoughts unnoticed. I don't recall what became of Ohana, but Reichan moved away to Kashiwazaki. Her father complained because he had not received the Order of the Golden Kite[3] and because he had been relegated to the regiment in the Kashiwazaki district. Reichan is the only one of these girls I will mention again.

All sorts came to attend the new middle school. In age they ranged from me, the youngest, to a boy who was twenty years old and had been sitting in his family's store since finishing upper elementary school three or four years earlier. Some came from among the shop boys in the villages. Others had flunked out of middle schools in Niigata or Nagaoka.

These older students introduced us to many things. No sooner had school begun than several of those who lived in dormitories took along six or eight of the fourteen-year-olds to a brothel. The school staff soon found out about it and expelled the older ones involved, putting a stop to that sort of thing.

Among the students, the most power was held by a gang of bullies who had drifted to Shibata from another school. Each member of the gang took a younger, good-looking boy to be his new friend. They exchanged oaths of brotherhood by cutting their fingers and drinking each other's blood. I knew nothing about such things during my first year, but toward the end of my second I did learn about it and took a "younger brother" of my own; but I didn't bother with cut fingers or drinking blood. This practice I continued for two or three years.

I also discovered smoking. Now and again I would steal one of the Chutengu brand cigarettes that Father always smoked. Ultimately I even got to the point of stealing and smoking the cigars my father prized so highly.

III.

About the time that I entered middle school, one of the teachers at the upper elementary school named Mr. Sakamoto opened the Academy of

3. See chapter 1 note 12.

Martial Arts, a judo hall built mainly with contributions from army men. Most of the sons of military families attended, including Ishikawa and Ōkubo. Also attending was a boy named Wakida. His father was a captain who was rumored to have hidden out in the mountains for a week during the battle of Weihaiwei.[4] After the triumphant return home, he had been immediately retired. His son was in our class in school but was two years older and fairly big. We played tricks on him because of his father. But then he himself told us that his real father was the Kanazawa man who had assassinated Ōkubo Toshimichi.[5] Hearing this as well as that he had ———, we began to have some respect for him. I, of course, attended the academy too.

I studied judo very diligently. There were sessions every day in the morning and the afternoon, and I hardly missed a day, especially during the midwinter session when we took our exercise outside in snow three feet deep. I had great success. After a year and a half or two years I became the demon boss of the group.

Every fall a festival was held at the Suwa Shrine and each neighborhood entered a float. A great deal of fighting went on between the floats. The Kaji Shopkeepers Association of Kaji-machi had lost during the last fight and, determined to have revenge the next year, ten of their members became pupils at the judo academy. All were shop boys around twenty years old, their arms with terrific bulging muscles as thick as our legs. The teacher chose me to be their opponent. Every time one of them grabbed my arm it hurt so badly that I thought the bone had broken. But their legs and hips were no stronger than ours; by taking advantage of this fact, I managed to throw one after another of them. Everyone else was delighted and the teacher made me his assistant. Then students would frequently give me a present such as a small knife.

4. See chapter 1 part 4 and accompanying note 11.
5. Ōkubo (1830–1878) was a central figure in the Meiji government until his assassination in 1878; his assailants were executed for their crime. The leader was Shimada Ichirō, a lower samurai from the castle town of Kanazawa in Ishikawa Prefecture, where the members of the band were "virtually canonized" for their bravery and sincerity (see Sidney D. Brown, "Political Assassination in Early Meiji Japan," 31). Perhaps because the text attributes heroism to the assassins, the censor has deleted a key noun.

I also studied the use of the staff and the rope.[6] The staff became my particular speciality. Even today I still have so much confidence in my ability with it that if I had one I would not even fear two or three policemen with drawn swords.

During my first summer vacation from the military cadet school, an old man named Morikawa who had been the teacher of Sakamoto, my teacher, sent a message for me. It said to come for a week to visit because he was going to bestow on me some special instruction. The old man lived on the seashore near Shidaihama, about five miles from Shibata, and I went partly because I wanted to swim at the beach. He wore his hair in an old-fashioned topknot and his back was stooped. As soon as I arrived he had me square off with the staff just as I had so many times before in the academy. He faced me with a thick wooden sword; I had a staff. His battle cries were so terrible that they sent shivers down my spine. Then he checked my staff with his wooden sword, steadily bearing down until I could no longer move my weapon.

The old man brought out a register written on a scroll. With his bad eyes, he said, he couldn't write himself, so he had me write. It was an exotic thing: there was a Marishiten[7] in the eastern corner and some other figure in the west; still others in the northern and in the southern corners, and an inscription written in syllabary that I couldn't understand but that looked like a magic formula or spell. After it came the register, a kind of genealogical chart, beginning with a Fujiwara somebody and a Minamoto whoever[8] and listing the names of ten or twenty persons to whom the scroll had been passed down. At the very end was the old man's name, Morikawa something-Bei, Esq., who had received it from Minamoto somebody. The old man told me to write Ōsugi Sakae, Esq., and I entered my name after his at the very end of the chart. He did not teach me the meaning of the inscription. But, saying that no

6. The *bō* (staff) and the *nawa* (rope) are traditional Japanese weapons.
7. Marishiten is a Buddhist deity sometimes associated with war.
8. These are two of the most famous aristocratic families of ancient and medieval Japan.

one must be permitted to see, the old man took me naked into his godown and taught me some judo holds.

Later, the old man came to see my father and made a nuisance of himself by wanting to teach the soldiers a magic spell to protect them against bullets. His style of judo was called the "new Araki style" though in fact it was a very old style.

Long afterward Sakamoto sent word that he was coming to Tokyo and would visit me. It was after I had finished my first jail term and had set up a household. I heard secondhand that he and my father had conferred and that Sakamoto would come in an attempt to influence me. But it was nothing like that. Even today he still visits frequently and reminisces about the old days. When he heard about my lung ailment, he was greatly surprised: "There is absolutely no reason for you to fall ill," he said, and advised me to practice some exercises he had invented called "uncoiling routines." Recently while in prison I've got a good deal of benefit from those exercises.

Sakamoto was about thirty when I first knew him, short and very round in stature. He must be over fifty now but still teaches judo at the gymnasium he built next to the Shuyō Academy in Koishikawa. He also teaches swimming in the summers around Koyasu and holds midwinter swim sessions every year near the Sumida River.

Sometime after I had started at the judo academy I took up the study of fencing with the bamboo sword. This kept me from the afternoon judo sessions so that I fell behind in judo. I have forgotten what the fencing style was called but the teacher's name was Imai.

Imai was a tall, fat roughneck who reinforced his big bamboo sword with several strands of wire like telegraph cable. He had the reputation of being a patriot of sorts and there was even a story that when Hoshi Tōru was on a speaking tour, Imai threw him and his carriage into the river.[9] More recently there was another story that Imai became so ag-

9. Hoshi (1850–1901), a flamboyant politician in the movement for freedom and popular rights and onetime Speaker of the House of Representatives, was involved in several bribery scandals. In a separate incident, a swordsman named Iba Sōtarō assassinated him.

itated at the unveiling of the statue of Ōkura Kihachirō that he rushed at Ōkura to strike him down but onlookers managed to stop him before he could fulfill his threat.[10]

Imai taught us rough stuff with the thick bamboo sword and consequently when at the military school we practiced fencing with thin toylike swords and fencing gloves it was really very boring.

While in middle school I had thrown myself into all sorts of strenuous exercise, including baseball. After running about all day, I ate huge meals. Every New Year's I stood up against a pillar in the house and we measured my height against last year's. Between my thirteenth and fourteenth New Year's I grew about six inches. I grew almost another five inches by my fifteenth New Year's and stood over five feet four inches tall.

IV.

The headmaster at the middle school was the Professor Miyoshi Aikichi who was made chief tutor to the imperial princess before his death a few years ago. We nicknamed him Confucius not only because he had a beard like Confucius but because he could never say anything without quoting Confucius. With a very solemn and serious expression he would lecture on morals from the *Analects*. One day in the beginning of my second year, he asked each of us in the ethics class to name someone we admired as our idol. Such men as Hideyoshi, Ieyasu, Masashige, and Kiyomaro[11] were named as my turn gradually came around.

Actually there was no one whom I idolized. I liked none of the men who occurred to me as possible choices. I tried to think of someone new but no one came to mind. When my turn finally came I was at a complete loss. Nevertheless, I stood up and as I did so suddenly recalled a book I had bought and read recently, somebody's essay on Saigō Nan-

10. See chapter 1 note 9.
11. Wake no Kiyomaro (733–799) and Kusonoki Masashige (1294–1336) were ministers renowned for their loyalty to the imperial throne in times of trouble. Toyotomi Hideyoshi (1568–1595) and Tokugawa Ieyasu (1542–1616) were warlords who reunified the country after the long feudal wars of the sixteenth century.

shu.[12] Trying to make a good impression, I answered: "Saigō Nanshu." After everyone had his turn, the teacher commented on each answer. In remarking on mine, he said, "Yes, of course, Saigō was one of the great men of modern times—possibly the greatest Japanese of modern times. But he was a rebel. He was a rebel who drew his bowstring against the emperor. And no matter what the circumstances were or however meritorious his other deeds, he cannot be forgiven for that. So, it goes without saying, it is inexcusable to admire him as an idol."

That's more or less the meaning of the teacher's criticism of my answer. Then the teacher extolled the virtues of Confucius, holding him up as the model of someone whom we all should admire as our idol.

I was very upset with the teacher's criticism. No mention that Saigō's rebellion had been against the emperor was in the book I had read. It had said that his rebellion was to flush out and drive away the corrupt officials from behind the scenes. I had believed this; yet since the teacher had spoken, it was no longer any good. There could no longer be any question of whether Saigō was justified or not. His greatness was flawed. Returning home, I reread his biography and came to admire him even more.

The biography of Saigō Nanshu led me to read biographies of Yoshida Shōin and Hirano Kuniomi.[13] I don't remember clearly which parts interested me most but after reading how Hirano traveled about raising troops, I liked him immensely.

Headmaster Miyoshi brought with him a teacher named Fukuda to be the head teacher. Fukuda was a short handsome man with a full beard. He was in charge of first-year English and ethics. In ethics class he used to go on and on about Lieutenant Gunji's going off to the Kurile Islands.[14] Fukuda's English pronunciation, unlike that of the elementary

12. This is Saigō Takamori (1827–1877), the hero of the wars of the Meiji Restoration who broke with the government in 1873 and led the last great samurai uprising in 1877, the so-called Satsuma rebellion. He was pardoned posthumously in 1891.

13. Yoshida (1830–1858) and Hirano (1828–1864) were both activists in the movement against the Tokugawa and inspired some of the heroes of the Meiji restoration.

14. A Lieutenant Gunji Naritada led a group to the Kurile Islands in 1893 as part of the government policy of settling the northern islands to prevent Russian encroachment.

school teachers or my private tutor, was very good and pleasant to listen to. But our science and natural history teacher, who had a university degree, was so ill-tempered that none of us could get very interested in science. My calligraphy teacher was an old man who always told me that I shouldn't be so careless when copying because the more carefully one copied a model the better one would be able to write. At the military school my calligraphy teacher told me the same thing. But no matter how I tried, I couldn't copy the strokes perfectly, and since I was so negligent in that class I cannot write properly even today. Nor could I draw. I can't begin to count all the pencil drawings and later brush paintings that I did in the first- and second-year classes and I still can't draw. It's something I hate.

Actually I never studied during middle school. English was the only subject in which I did excel; in all the rest I scored B's. Even so, I was in the upper third of my class.

Torakō graduated from upper elementary school at the same time that I finished my first year in middle school. He lived alone with his grandmother. They were so poor that I don't know how they managed even to eat. Though Torakō had his heart set on entering middle school, it seemed utterly impossible; I felt very sorry for him. Finally I devised a plan and told him about it. I would give him the old books I had used and if his uncle would give him the money for tuition, he could go.

Overjoyed, Torakō talked to his grandmother and then went immediately to ask his uncle, who was the prison warden. Torakō's fate, however, had already been decided. He came home from his uncle's in tears. Scolding Torakō for being so impudent as to want to continue in school, his uncle had ordered him to go to Hokkaido to become a clerk in a shop in the city of Hakodate.

There wasn't anything I could do to help him. The two of us put our arms around each other and wept, saying that I would become a general and he would become a great merchant. We swore that we would be friends forever; we had our picture taken together as a memento. I had my mother make him a suit of warm flannel underwear as a going-away present.

I have failed to become a general, but I wonder how Torakō is doing. His full name is Nishimura Torakō.

Just after Torakō left, I took the entrance examination for military cadet school. I had autographed the back of our picture, A Future Field Marshal. But I didn't study for the examination and failed miserably.

V.

That summer I took my first trip by myself. I planned at first to go only as far as Tokyo and started out with just ten yen.[15] Still it turned into a grand tour as I went on to Nagoya and Osaka.

The railroad in Echigo had reached only as far as the city of Naoetsu, so I took the boat from Niigata to Naoetsu. It was the first occasion that I can actually recall seeing a steamship or a train, much less riding on one. Uncle Yamada met me in Tokyo.

He was a colonel and the commanding officer of one regiment of the Imperial Guard. He had bought the mansion of a General Ōdera who had been killed at the battle of Weihaiwei. The house had just been finished. My uncle patted me on the head, commenting, "You did quite well to travel here all by yourself." He acted fonder of me than my own father usually did. Aunt Yamada also continually called, "Sakae, Sakae," and could hardly stay away.

There were two cousins. The younger, Tetsu, had dropped out of an advanced course at the Peers School because of illness and had gone to Shinano Prefecture for practical training in sericulture. The maids referred to him as "the young master." The elder brother, Ryō, had just become a first lieutenant and lived in a separate house in the back with his pretty bride, Oshige. He was an instructor at the Army Officer Academy and was making preparations to enter the Military Staff College.

The maids called me the "young master from Echigo" and whenever I said or did anything they would bury their faces in their sleeves and laugh. Although Oshige glared at them, they couldn't help it; I was so funny. A Western-style banquet would be served but the "young master from Echigo" would have no idea how to eat it. There were no Western-

15. This sum was worth about five U.S. dollars at the time.

style restaurants in Shibata yet and I had never eaten such food at home. At last, imitating the others, I took my knife and cut a piece of beefsteak. I put it into my mouth but I had cut a piece far too large—my mouth was so full that I couldn't chew or swallow it. Everyone laughed, even Oshige. I shall never forget the sight of her face laughing at me.

I thought Oshige the greatest beauty in all Japan. Oshige's older sister was also beautiful. She was married to a cavalry lieutenant studying at the Military Staff College. I resolved to study diligently so that next year I could pass the entrance examination for the military cadet school and someday attend the Military Staff College.

I also went to visit Oshige's family, the Suekawas, at their home in Itakura.[16] I, who had been intoxicated by the comforts of the Yamada house, was stupefied when I saw how many times more luxurious was the Suekawa home. There were two houses, the main residence and down from it a separate house. Suekawa had only one child by his wife, his first son, who wasn't very bright. The other sons and daughters, including Oshige, were the children of a concubine who was said to be from Karasumori. All the children of this woman were attractive. The two younger girls lived with their mother in the separate house. Though she was in fact their mother, all the children called the concubine simply by her name, Eichan.[17]

At meal times everyone usually gathered at the main house, where the sons lived. There was a Western-style drawing room in the main house, and when I visited the house I went in to lie down on the Western-style sofa. It was at this house that I also saw my first telephone and at Oshige's house that I first heard the sound of a piano. Despite the grace and beauty of all members of the family, I somehow felt a coldness about them. It, however, did not prevent me from visiting them frequently to savor the luxury of their life.

16. When these relatives are mentioned again in chapter 6 part 4, both the 1930 Kaizō and 1957 Chikuma editions give the place-name as "Iigura"; since their first Chinese characters are similar, the one is probably a typographical error for the other.

17. *Eichan* is the diminutive form, which makes Ōsugi's point more obvious. The arrangement would not have been completely out of the ordinary for an upper-class Japanese family of the day.

The Suekawas were a branch family of a Kagoshima family who had served as ministers to their domain lord.[18] I heard that the husband had formerly been a finance officer or something in the navy and was at this time in private business. It was said that when the Yamada family was first approached concerning a possible marriage, it hesitated because Oshige was the daughter of a concubine. But a high-ranking officer, either Admiral Kawamura or General Takashima,[19] intervened and the Yamadas were forced to accept the match. Afterward, the children of Ryō and Oshige would often visit the home of Admiral Kawamura when the current crown prince and his brothers were there, returning home with toy bears or elephants and other presents.

Ryō is now a major general and the commander of a brigade somewhere. Tanaka, the husband of Oshige's sister, is a lieutenant general and now in Washington as an army representative at the Pacific Conference.[20] Uncle Yamada finally reached the rank of lieutenant general and is now living in retirement in Wakayama.

While on this trip I also visited my father's relatives in Nagoya and my mother's in Osaka. They were all either in farming or business and their homes were quite plain. Since they weren't the least bit interesting, I returned to Tokyo and spent another month enjoying myself there.

VI.

My first experience in handling money came on that trip. Until then I had never had a single coin in pocket money; when I needed something I would charge it at the store. After the trip I could no longer be satisfied with that arrangement.

18. These were high-ranking retainers of the Satsuma domain, from which came many of the civilian as well as military elite in the Meiji period.

19. These were probably General Viscount Takashima Tomonosuke (1844–1916) and Admiral Count Kawamura Sumiyoshi (1836–1904), both prominent natives of Kagoshima. Takashima became Minister of the Army in the late 1890s and Kawamura served as a Privy Councillor. Later in 1901 Kawamura received the honor of serving as Guardian of the Imperial Princes, so the crown prince mentioned below was the Shōwa Emperor, who reigned from 1926 to 1989.

20. Lieutenant General Tanaka Kunishige (1869–1941) attended the 1921–22 Washington conference.

The new middle school had been built among a long row of cryptomeria trees on the road between Shibata and Ijimino. At the end of the
row of trees was a small restaurant called the Hebizukaya. Our gang
called it by the English word *Snake*.[21] All of us often would cut class to
go there so it was the scene of a great deal of mischief. Because of this
I began stealing money out of my mother's purse. She was always putting her purse somewhere and forgetting where. When she needed
money she had to search the whole house, so she seldom knew how
much she had in the purse. I took advantage of this to take small sums
from time to time.

As time went on, these sums weren't enough and I finally sold the
watch my father had given me. He had owned it for a long time. It was
a very old-fashioned one in a silver case with a key that you put in a hole
in the back and wound noisily. Mother found out somehow and told
me, "Take that watch and go to your father's room." No longer pos-
sessing the watch, I had no choice but to go empty-handed and prepared
for a severe scolding.

Father began the court proceedings. I answered only that I had sold
the watch. I couldn't say what I had done with the money because I was
afraid if I told Father about the *Snake* he would then find out about the
other mischief—particularly about such things as the brotherhood
among students in the gang. Both of my parents scolded me harshly and
hit me, but I wouldn't tell them anything more.

During that winter we heard from the leaders of our gang—now
third- and fourth-year students—that something momentous had happened. The Association Assembly had censured Headmaster Miyoshi
and voted to dismiss him.

The middle school had been built by an association consisting of Shibata and the forty-some villages surrounding the town. The association
had an assembly and it was this Association Assembly that had passed
the vote of no confidence. Occasionally matters concerning the operation of the school were raised in the assembly and we heard that there

21. Ōsugi gives it the English name *suneku;* the full name of the restaurant was the
Shop of the Grave of the Snake.

had been some kind of proposal concerning educational policy. We also heard that the headmaster had flatly rejected it. We knew nothing about what kind of proposal had been made. Neither did we know any of the contents of the vote of censure. Nor did we know any of the circumstances in which the association had become entangled. Nevertheless, we decided that the association was at fault. We resolved to start a movement in support of the headmaster.

A mass meeting of students was held the next day at the Chōtokuji Temple with all the second-, third-, and fourth-year students there (the first-year students, being unable yet to understand such things, were purposely excluded from membership). The entire gathering voted unanimously to link our fate with Headmaster Miyoshi. The commotion continued for a month, right up until the approach of school examinations. It was then decided to turn the general boycott into a mass withdrawal from school.

Saying that a school like this was no longer any use, someone smashed the glass doors to pieces. Then almost all the desks and chairs in the classrooms were broken up into the size of firewood for the stove. One of the teachers, driving his carriage through the parade grounds at night, was beaten up because it was said that he was in league with the association.

One day my parents called me to where they were sitting next to the charcoal fire in the living room. "I understand that there is some kind of trouble and you haven't been to school at all lately," Father said. He had heard about it from the information that the association had sent to all the students' parents and guardians. It blamed the headmaster and asked that all the students be sent back to school the next day.

I muttered, as if to myself, that I wouldn't go. Father leaped to his feet, but Mother calmed him, begging, "This child won't listen to anything you tell him. Please forget the matter for now."

The commotion ended with the association withdrawing its vote of censure, the headmaster giving his resignation, and, at his entreaty, the students being given their final examinations.

Headmaster Miyoshi and his assistant Fukuda moved on together to a middle school in Nagano. A farewell party was held for them in a restaurant in Naka-machi. The headmaster was a great drinker and everyone at the party drank a bottle of sake apiece. Throughout the party there was a smile on the headmaster's square face and Fukuda, in his esteemed voice, recited a poem about the "Band of White Tigers" who were from his hometown.[22]

When it was finally time for the headmaster to leave town, the entire student body of three hundred marched off with his sled in the center through the high drifts of snow twenty miles to Niigata.

Miyoshi's successor was Hirota Ichijō. Despite the fact that his name sounded as if he should have been a priest, he was a stylish fellow who had just received his bachelor's degree.[23] Shortly after he arrived he did some sort of experiment in the art of memory at a meeting of the school supporters and this actually made him unpopular with the pupils. Then he did something else. It was customary for the students to take off their shoes before entering the place where the portrait of the emperor was kept but it was said that he had entered with his shoes still on. This touched off a serious movement to dismiss him.

That spring I took the military school entrance examination for the second time. On the very first day I almost failed the physical. I had had no trouble with the eye chart the year before, but this time everything below the first two or three lines was a blur. I couldn't make out one part from another.

The young medical officer, shaking his head, went into the other room to call a second army doctor. This was Dr. Hiraga, who had taken care of my illnesses since I was a small child. He said, "He's got to get in this year, whatever it is," and he corrected the eye examination. Then he took me off into a dark room and had me try on several pairs of glasses. In the end, I cleared the physical.

---

22. In Aizu in 1868, during the civil war that accompanied the overthrow of the Tokugawa regime and the establishment of the Meiji government, a group of young samurai known as the *byakkotai* (white tigers) defended their castle against the Restorationist forces. In the end, some sixteen between the ages of fifteen and seventeen years threw themselves on their swords rather than surrender.

23. *Ichijō* is written with the characters for "single vehicle" and thus refers to the teachings of Buddha. Since only a small segment of the populace held the bachelor's degree, it carried considerable prestige.

Although I had not studied for it, the entrance examination was about at the level of upper elementary school and I didn't have trouble with it.

A little before the official results were to be announced, we received a telegram from Uncle Yamada: "CONGRATULATIONS ON SAKAE'S ADMISSION."

CHAPTER 4

CADET SCHOOL

1899-1901

I.

The Central Military Preparatory School was in Tokyo, but at that time there was a district cadet school[1] at each of the six army division headquarters. The central school taught the main curriculum while the district schools taught preliminary courses. Each student attended in his family's home district. For example, those whose families were registered in the district of the First Division attended the district school of the division headquartered in Tokyo. After having the military spirit instilled in them at a district school for three years, all students went on to the central school in Tokyo. Since my family was registered originally in Nagoya, I went to the Nagoya district school.[2]

---

1. Thomas Stanley translates *yōnen gakkō*, the chapter title here, as "Kadet School." For his reasoning, which I find quite sound, see his *Ōsugi Sakae,* 177 n.1. Nevertheless, I prefer to spell the term with *c,* partly because as a French student Ōsugi would have known the term originated with the *école des cadets* and partly because *k* might strike some readers as even more Kafkaesque than he intended. In any case, references to *yōnen* schools are not to be confused with the next levels up, the Rikugun Shikan Gakkō (Army Officer Academy) or the Rikugun Daigaku (Military Staff College). One of the best English sources on the military education system is Theodore Failor Cook Jr., "The Japanese Army Officer Corps," esp. 40–43.

2. In the system of census registration in force then for all Japanese, civilian and military alike, Nagoya was listed in Ōsugi's register (*honseki*) as the geographic origin of his household though his family was then domiciled in Shibata.

Later my father would blame my becoming a Socialist on the fact that I studied French. He had a vague idea that France was the country of revolution. I agree in part, but for more clearly defined reasons. As a matter of fact, though, I began French at military school because I was assigned to that class. French and German were both taught at the Tokyo district school while schools in other districts offered Russian as well as French and German. Applicants for admission indicated on their applications which of these languages they preferred to study. Because it was said that French was behind the times and German was the language of the future, I selected German. My father became my tutor, though not a good one, and we spent a month going through a first reader.

On the way to Nagoya I stopped in Tokyo to visit Ōkubo, who had moved to the capital a year or two before. He also had failed the previous year and had made it into the district school in Tokyo only that year. Moreover he too intended to study German. Ishikawa, who was already studying at the Kumamoto district school, also came to Tokyo on vacation. While I was there, the three of us got together. Ishikawa was really very good at German and he was scathing in his condemnation of French. Ōkubo and I looked through his German book and the two of us were very envious, though neither of us could make head or tail out of its queer script.

The very first thing the staff did on the opening day of school was to take the fifty new students into the fencing hall and line us up according to height. The second thing they did was to decide what language each of us was to study. The school policy was to divide us into two equal groups: in other words, twenty-five to study German and twenty-five to study French. But there were far more applicants for German than for French. The captain in charge stood very tall like a German officer, his chest out, his back straight, and his left hand resting on his hip. With his right hand he twisted his moustache while he spoke.

"Those who have been studying German up to now and wish to continue will, of course, be permitted to. But you will have to have learned more than just the alphabet or *es ist*. We will give you an examination."

There were three or four others beside myself who didn't know much more than *es ist* and everyone was frightened into silence by the mention of an examination. But then the captain must have changed his mind, because without further delay he divided us into German and French groups.

My name fell into the French group. I was disappointed. It was an order, however, and therefore nothing could be done about it. Besides, I had always liked languages and enjoyed French from the first. Since the other courses were just reviews of what I had done in middle school, I concentrated all my efforts on French.

The textbook, *French Book*, had been published in America and had footnotes in English. I couldn't pronounce French properly but I read ahead on my own by consulting the footnotes and constantly referring to a large French-Japanese dictionary. At the beginning of the second or third school term, the teacher handed out dictionaries entirely in French. Doing as he told us to, we used them exclusively, whether or not we understood what was written in them. At the same time he gave us the dictionaries, he passed out to each student an old French children's magazine. He said, "It doesn't matter whether you understand or don't understand. Just keep reading." That was this teacher's motto. I faithfully read the magazine I had received from beginning to end two or three times. In doing so, I grew quite familiar with the French dictionary and eventually began to be able to figure out more or less what this children's magazine was about.

On my first Saturday at school, a few days after arrival, a third-year student who was looking after me said that the next day I was to attend a meeting at the clubhouse of my "province."[3] I didn't really have the slightest concept of "province." I knew nothing about Marugame, the place in Sanuki province where I was born. My family was registered in Owari, but neither did I know it well. Moreover, I had seldom even heard the term. In Shibata, where I had been until then, almost every-

3. Japanese readers would have been quite amused by the youthful Ōsugi's confusion about the term *kuni*. It literally means "province" but is also, as here, "native place." A province was a division of ancient Japan and must be distinguished from both Tokugawa domains and modern prefectures. Sanuki (or Sanshū) was merely a section of Kagawa Prefecture on the island of Shikoku; Owari was part of Aichi Prefecture of which the city of Nagoya was capital, whereas Echigo was in Niigata Prefecture.

body was from Shibata or that area. Like everybody else, I referred to myself as a son of north Echi. But I never thought of Echigo province as my province.

Thus when the upperclassman spoke of the clubhouse of my province, I wasn't clear about his meaning. Yet you must always listen very carefully to anything that a superior officer or upperclassman said—this was the very first thing you were taught. I saluted the upperclassman and stood at attention whenever he said anything at all to me. Thus I now gave him a proper salute, answering only, "Yes, sir." Seeing how nervous I was, the upperclassman said with a kind expression on his face, "The lord of our province has made it possible, so we all go there on Sundays and enjoy ourselves."

Actually, this word "lord" sounded just as strange to me.[4] Like province, it was a word that evoked no feelings in me. Of course, Shibata had a lord and I had often heard the title, but it didn't move me to feelings of veneration or gratitude. A year or so before, the lord and his lady had come to Shibata from Tokyo on the thirtieth anniversary of something and as they passed through the streets the smell of musk and perfume was so absurdly strong that I had to hold my nose. The only impression I had was a disagreeable one. Nonetheless, I felt happy to hear that the meeting place on Sunday was made possible by the lord.

The clubhouse was a temple near the school. Forty or fifty students, new and upperclassmen, gathered in a room in the main building.

"First of all, you must band together in a tight group with your comrades from your province. You must fulfill your chief mission as cadets here as part of this band. And you must never permit yourselves to be humiliated by those from other provinces."

These "instructions" were delivered by a short but powerfully built fellow named Yamada, who had a left shoulder about a foot higher than the right. As I listened to him, I was reminded of Inoue, whom I considered the most outstanding leader of the middle-school gang in Shibata. He finished by saying, "And all here shall be companions." These words moved me very much.

4. *Tonosama* is a generic term of respect that refers here to the former daimyo, the head of the Mizoguchi family who had controlled a minor domain until the 1870s.

After Yamada's "instructions" came those of four or five others. In essence all came down to the same point: "You must never permit yourselves to be humiliated by those from other provinces." We were told that in the senior—the third-year—class there were about ten students each from Ishikawa Prefecture and Aichi Prefecture and that the two groups were striving against each other for supremacy. The Aichi Prefecture students in the next class, the second-year students, were slightly more numerous. In my class of first-year students the Aichi Prefecture men totaled twenty-six, an absolute majority. Yet we couldn't become complacent just because we were more numerous; if we were defeated despite our numbers then the loss would be all the more shameful. Therefore we had to be united.

I didn't understand what the Aichi and Ishikawa students had to fight about. Nevertheless, I was extraordinarily happy to enter this group where I knew no one but where we could immediately, being from the same province, become such special friends. Without further cause I began to hate Ishikawa students as the enemies of my new friends.

After the "instructions," refreshments were served. Out came a box overflowing with sweet rice cakes from a local confectionery. After we had eaten those, there was quite an abundance of sake wine. We gorged ourselves. Even I, who had never been able to drink much sake, got carried away in the party's high spirits and piled up quite a few empty cups in front of me. Then, much to our surprise, Yamada and some of the other "companions" began to recite Chinese verse with homosexual allusions.[5] Thus it was that I became "companions" with Yamada and the others.

II.

The third-year students were extremely hard on the students in the class immediately below theirs—that is, the second-year students—but were kind to the first-year students. After I became a member of their group, these veterans made me one of their favorite "companions"—perhaps even more favored than the others. If you were a "companion" of these

5. The specific verse was "Tsung tz'u miao ling chin ch'eng chang." On homosexuality in civilian boarding schools see Roden, *Schooldays in Imperial Japan*.

veterans, you could get away with anything, no matter how wrong. Smoking, for instance, was a guardhouse offense if you were caught. But they had a special place where it was safe. The veterans from Aichi at first hesitated to take me there, but some of those from other provinces—especially Tokyo—took me along with them from the beginning.

It was also these third-year students from Tokyo who taught me something else—something punishable at least by detention or, even more seriously, by expulsion from school. At night after everyone else was asleep, they took me along when they went to amuse themselves in the sleeping quarters of those on the left flank.[6] This was the most serious business in which "companions" took part.

Among the veterans who came from Tokyo was one who wasn't a "companion." This was the son of General Nogi.[7] He was the largest boy in the senior class and the worst at his studies. He had a large mouth that always seemed to be grinning.

I wasn't always engaged in the "vices of bushido." I also made real progress in true bushido. The head teacher, who had a bachelor's degree in letters,[8] lectured on bushido in the ethics course. He said that the soul of bushido was the choice of the right way to die. I was deeply impressed. I thus made a resolution that, in order to fulfill bushido, I would not fail to choose in advance how I would die. I began to do research on the ways in which the samurai of old had died. Whenever I found something in a book, I would copy it down verbatim. My notes eventually filled a volume of their own.

6. The entering class of students was evidently grouped into thirds, starting with the tallest on the right flank; those on the "left flank" would be the smaller students. Ōsugi's place was in the right flank. I omit other divisions by school semester within each year's class unless they are necessary to understand the narrative.

7. The father, Nogi Maresuke (1849–1912), was already a national hero for his command of the victorious infantry brigade in the Liaotung Peninsula during the Sino-Japanese War (see chapter 2 note 7) and gained further fame in the Russo-Japanese War of 1904–5 and as president of the Peers School. By the time of this work Nogi had become a legend for his ritual suicide at the death of his sovereign, the Meiji emperor. Presumably the son was one of Nogi's two sons killed in the war against Russia.

8. His degree was in *bungaku*. Often translated as "literature," *bungaku* involved a much broader array of subjects in Japanese colleges, including philosophy and history. A bachelor's degree carried considerable prestige in the 1890s.

Of all those examples of death, the one that most moved me was the story of the crucifixion of Torii Suneimon in the period of the Warring States.[9] In fact, more inspiring than the story was the inscription someone had written on the picture of his crucifixion: "To die with patriotic fervor is easy—to meet death with tranquillity is difficult." I folded my arms and swore to myself, I will show them that I too can die with tranquillity.

I remember something else about the teacher I just mentioned. It concerned his explanation of the word "redress" in the Imperial Rescript on the Retrocession of the Liaotung Peninsula. I don't remember now what came before or after but the phrase probably went something like "Nursing our grievances, we seek redress."[10] Whatever the ostensible meaning of "redress," he said that it actually meant "revenge." Even today I cannot remember what the ostensible meaning was supposed to be, so welcome did I find this real meaning.

I've forgotten what month—probably toward the beginning of the summer—there was a holiday to commemorate the capture of Pyongyang.[11] Breakfast that day was the first time I had been served what they called millet gruel. It was slightly sweet and, I thought, rather good. The side dishes were small amounts of green soybeans and tinned beef. This breakfast repast was served throughout the entire Third Division.

The officer of the day, Captain Kitagawa, whom I've also mentioned earlier,[12] spoke to us in the dining room about the story behind this repast: it was the same meal the troops had eaten in celebration on either the morning or the evening of the day Pyongyang was captured.

After we finished eating, we assembled in the lecture hall. On the front wall was hung a large map of Asia. The Liaotung Peninsula in China was colored red, the same color as Japan. All the officers and staff

9. In the *Sengoku* period from the mid-fifteenth to the late sixteenth centuries, war was endemic in Japan.

10. Stanley's somewhat more literal and perhaps more accurate translation is "We shall endure hardship and privation and will devise our retaliation" (*Ōsugi Sakae*, 3).

11. It was on 16 September 1894 that Japanese troops took this heavily fortified city from its Chinese defenders and achieved control of the Korean peninsula only weeks after the Sino-Japanese War began.

12. This is the first mention of this captain's name; he is apparently the one who had divided the new students into language groups.

from the school were in attendance and the head teacher, whom I was discussing above, gave his lecture about "redress." When the head teacher's lecture was over, we were led off to a town east of Nagoya, this time to a military cemetery. Here were the many tombstones of the teachers' comrades-in-arms and we stopped by every stone, one by one, to listen to Captain Kitagawa and the other school officers reminisce. Each concluded with the necessity of waging war on Russia, the ringleader of the Triple Intervention, to take revenge: "For the sake of the departed souls of these brave soldiers, we must take up arms and obtain revenge." We all felt our blood boil within us.

One day not long after I had returned to Shibata for my first midsummer holidays, I happened to open the drawer in my father's desk and spotted an envelope with the word [SECRET] stamped on the outside.[13] The seal had already been broken so I opened it and looked. It was addressed to the commanding officers of all the divisions and brigades from ———, the chief—or perhaps it was vice chief—of the General Staff. These were orders regarding the education of officers and troops, saying something to the effect that ———. I read the dates and counted on my fingers. If it was ——— then I should be a second lieutenant at that time. I jumped for joy.

On top of Father's desk were a Russian language book and a magazine from the Amur River Society.[14] (As I write this, I have a suspicion that this event might have taken place before I entered military school, for I seem to recall it was in Father's room at the house in Katata-machi. My father had begun serving as brigade adjutant about then. We had moved to Onoue-machi either the year before or the same year that I entered military school. Then this must have been something that happened at Onoue-machi. If that is so, then I have reversed the memories to put this one after, when actually it comes before the memory of having learned about redress vis-à-vis Russia. Nevertheless, it remains a fact that I rejoiced when I read ——— and realized that I would be a second

13. The 1930 edition has deleted the word (464).
14. The Kokuryūkai (translated also as the more sinister sounding Black dragon society) lobbied actively for Japanese expansion on the continent and war against Russia.

lieutenant by then. Yet I never told a soul, keeping my joy and what I had learned about this [secret] within my heart alone.)

III.

I had entered military school ranked tenth or so in the class. As a result of the first-year examinations I moved up to eighth place. After middle school, however, I stopped competing for top honors. I decided that the first- or second-rank students were stupid, boorish bookworms. To myself I bragged, "Actually I have more ability than they do," and was perfectly satisfied with seventh or eighth place. Therefore, there wasn't much need to study for my courses, and, except for my interest in language class—which, as I said before, I liked—I didn't study.

When it came to brute strength or toughness, however, and the power that results from those, I was second to none from the very outset. I was actually only fourteenth or fifteenth from the right flank in height and by no means the strongest in my class. But that is a vastly different matter from toughness or power. Moreover, behind me I had the Aichi men, who constituted an absolute majority.

As a "companion" of the veteran students, I acted with arrogant disdain toward my own classmates. I didn't get along very well with those in my own sleeping quarters, but there were no complaints from those in the sleeping quarters of the left flank, where I often went for amusement. In the center sleeping quarters, there was a student named Nakamura. He was from Tokyo and had a quick tongue and a vitality about him. This fellow griped a lot about my playing around with the student who had the bed next to his. Two or three others also started to talk about it. So one night, after he did something, I took a swing at him in his sleeping quarters before everybody. He just rolled up his sleeves without a word and laughed as I punched him. At that, we immediately became friends. This Nakamura was to die of lung disease. His younger brother, Tsune, entered school during my fifth semester. He is the Nakamura Tsune who became the Western-style painter.[15]

15. Nakamura Tsune (1888–1924) was a prominent artist and also died of lung disease.

Among those in sleeping quarters for the right flank who were taller than I were a Kōno and a Satō. Since both Kōno and Satō came from a military prep school called Buyo in Nagoya, they had a lot of friends; most of those whose province was Nagoya were their friends. Among that group they were very close with two—Hamamura and Sakata, who were also on my right in the row. Kōno and Satō acted as though I were an enemy but Hamamura and Sakata took strange attitudes toward me and I could not tell whether they were enemies or allies. Any single one would make a dangerous adversary and I wouldn't be able to handle it if so many joined forces. So I quickly called Hamamura and Sakata aside and told them, "I'm going to have a duel with those two, Satō and Kōno, so you'd better decide where you stand." Both declared their neutrality. First I challenged the bigger of the two, Satō. He was the largest fellow in my class and the best at fencing. We went together into the gymnasium. When we got below the metal bars, I hit him by surprise. My fist struck him full in the eye; holding his eye with tears streaming down his face, he stood there silently. Hamamura and Sakata, being concerned, had come to watch. Both joined my side. Kōno soon paid me a friendly visit. After that, the five of us formed a gang and became partners in all sorts of wicked things.

Four or five years ago Satō came to visit me. Told that there was a childhood friend at the front door, I went to see who it could be. There he was, as tall as ever but now with a full growth of beard. He told me some story about getting into an argument with a regimental commander and being put on the reserve list. Now he had been forced out altogether. He said something about envying me now and, since we had been expelled together from school, wanted to ask my help in finding a job. He had been doing something connected with the administration of emigration to South America, but something had gone wrong. While he was telling me his story, my glance happened to fall on the red scar, exactly where I had hit him in the eye years before.

In fencing I was second only to Satō, and in other physical activities the three of us—Satō, Kōno, and I—were closely matched. But in running I was the fastest by far. Running was also the speciality of our squad leader, Master Sergeant Kawai; to his great chagrin he could never keep up with me.

Every day after classes the teachers had us play sports. Often we played European football or held tug-of-war matches. Our squad leader had difficulty in dividing us into teams. First he matched the front rank against the rear. But every time we played, the front rank—my side— won. Then he sent me to play with the rear rank. This time the rear rank won. He tried dividing us according to language class, having the French students play against the German students. But once again my side, the French, won. Sometimes he gave up and just took me out of the game, saying, "You, you watch from the sidelines."

What gave me trouble, however, was swimming. The first summer we went to the seacoast at Karasu on the Ise Peninsula for training. The teacher was an old man who was famous for the Kankai or some such style of swimming; it was said that when he was young he often swam from Ise across to Owari on the Chita Peninsula just to buy a bowl of miso soup. There were students from Ise who had swum eight and even ten miles using the Kankai style. Satō, who was our number one swimmer, used the same style. Most of the others from Nagoya also swam in this style.

I had spent a lot of time playing on the beach and in the river when I was a child, yet except to splash around and make a lot of noise I couldn't swim a stroke. I was really dumbfounded. In the first day's test, trying with all my might, I managed to swim five or six yards. I was put last in the C group. Veterans and first-year students served as assistant coaches and they taught us the Kankai style by holding our ankles and having us kick like frogs. I hated to have them hold my legs and every time I tried the style I got cramps. So I got away from the rest and practiced my own private style of dog paddle. When they tested us again at the end of the first week I dog-paddled a thousand meters and was promoted to A group. In the final test at the end of the second week, I swam farther than I ever had, four thousand meters still using the dog paddle. They named me one of the assistants for the next year.

That next year we went to Ōno on the Chita Peninsula. Though I was supposed to be an assistant, I couldn't teach the Kankai or any other style. I let the students I had charge of in C group simply play around in the water. But in the final test one of them swam four thousand yards using my style of dog paddle. He was a fourth-term student, still just a child, who was a special favorite of mine. He always seemed on the verge of tears during the tests so I continually shouted encouragement from the side to pull him through. Starting really from zero, this boy made such progress that he was the one praised as having made the most improvement that year.

Recently I ran into this fellow on a train. He had become a splendid officer and wore the staff insignia. At first I didn't notice him even though he was right in front of me. Only when he handed me his card, asking, "I wonder if you remember me?" did I recognize him. He spoke in the formal manner that senior officers have and although then he was only a captain, by now he is probably a major.

IV.

I became even more unruly in my second year at school. At the same time, there were now other fellows who could force me to bow my head. These were former second-year classmen who could for the first time hold up their heads as seniors. The year before I had buttoned my overcoat up over my head and gone with my senior "companions" when they raided the sleeping quarters of the second year's left flank. I too had laughed at these second-year classmen for being "youngsters." Such things had quite infuriated the leaders of the second-year class. One of these youngsters was from Ishikawa and now the Ishikawa students especially viewed me as their adversary.

They insisted that the second-year classmen from my own province punish me, citing all the times that I had been "impudent." The leader among my "companions" in the second-year class was named Asano. But he could do nothing to stop the others. Moreover, there were fellows among the second-year class from my province who secretly hated me. As a result I got a good beating. They made me stand at attention in the middle of a large group while they took turns punching me. The Ishikawa students also took their turn.

While being disciplined I could not raise a hand to protect myself—to do so would be insubordination against an upperclassman. As I was struck I remained still, mainly careful to keep my feet. I feared being kicked if I fell. Being hit with fists was not so bad. I stayed as calm as I could, counting each blow as it landed on my stomach. As long as I could keep the count I could endure it no matter how hard they punched. But I knew I wouldn't be able to hold out if they came at me all at once so that I couldn't tell one punch from another or, even worse, if they started to kick me from all sides. Actually, some were already doing so and, unable to defend myself, I could only stand at attention and glare at them.[16]

I used the term squad leaders earlier. These were noncommissioned officers who assisted the officers in charge and supervised the students, one master sergeant and one sergeant for each class. I was Master Sergeant Kawai's pet and he usually just winked at the things I did. He often caught me in some infraction but he would merely shout at me and never once did he turn me in to a superior officer. But before long Sgt. Kawai was transferred and his place was taken by an extremely tall, thin master sergeant. This new sergeant would walk about the study room with a mysterious notebook, peering back and forth from the notebook to our faces. Once I stole a look at this notebook. It had a list of words like *bravery, unruliness, nobility,* and *ignobility.* Below them were written two or three lines of explanation. The master sergeant was determining the character of each of us according to these terms.

As soon as he arrived, the master sergeant began to watch me with a strange look in his eye. Before he arrived the squad leader named Inakuma had always been so gentle that we had nicknamed him Sgt. Garçon or Sgt. Sonny. Now he suddenly became ill-tempered. The two of these sergeants tailed me constantly and reported everything I did to the officer in charge.

The result, of course, was invariably restriction to quarters. Every week I was restricted to quarters on Sunday. It was always for sticking

16. Roden describes a "clenched-fist" punishment in the boarding schools for civilian elites in *Schooldays in Imperial Japan,* 147–50.

dirty socks back into the drawer or sitting on the bed during daylight or something else so ridiculous that I can no longer remember what.

The noncommissioned officers had a room on the second floor immediately across from our sleeping quarters. The sergeants alternated weeks in charge of our sleeping quarters at night, but they would sleep below. When we were out of tobacco, we would sneak at night into their room on the second floor and steal some. One day we were all out of tobacco. First Kōno went to steal some. Next I went. I entered the room and had just put my hand in the drawer when someone shouted, "Hold it!" and grabbed me. It was the sergeant on duty, Sgt. Inakuma. He dragged me straight away to the room of the officer in charge, Lt. Yoshida.

"This is not the first time this has happened—for some days now, and even longer, tobacco has been disappearing from my desk. And yesterday some of my money disappeared. Today I decided to catch the culprit for sure and so I was waiting for him. Consequently, when I spotted this Ōsugi sneaking into the room, I caught him and brought him here." Triumphantly the sergeant reported to Lt. Yoshida. This first lieutenant was in charge of my class. Being from my province, he was the single officer who treated me as a favorite. Now he turned a bit pale and told the sergeant to go and write a full report of the incident. After the sergeant had left, Lt. Yoshida interrogated me. I persisted in denying that I was a thief.

"I never stole any tobacco—much less any money. I lost a button off my trousers today, so this evening I went to that room thinking there might be one there I could have."

"Where are these trousers you're talking about?"

"They're the ones I have on now." I showed him the place the button was missing—the button I had pulled off myself while being dragged in by the sergeant. The lieutenant grunted and nodded his head. Then he was silent for a while as if thinking. Of course, stealing anything—whether tobacco or money—meant expulsion. Even if I had lost a button, entering an off-limits area at night without permission inevitably meant the guardhouse. Even if that were the only punishment, the report would have to include the accusation by the noncommissioned officer. This accusation would be on my record for the future. Moreover, it was his responsibility. Finally he called the sergeant back and said these things for me to hear also. He asked the sergeant, for the sake of my future, to tear up the report. Grudgingly, the sergeant consented.

After that the sergeant and master sergeant kept me under even closer surveillance.

V.

The first lieutenant somebody or other who was in charge of one section within the second-year class had taken no interest in me since I was not his responsibility. But Captain Kitagawa, who had responsibility for another section of the second-year students, had disliked me intensely since he had been in charge of me during my first term. When I met him in the yard, I came to attention and saluted in the prescribed manner, stopping just six feet in front of him and raising my hand to my cap. He would scowl at me for a time and then proceed to criticize the position of my hand on the visor of my cap or something else. After that he would scrutinize my dress. If he found even one button missing from my coat or trousers, he would immediately confine me to quarters the following Sunday. Or, if it was one of those rare days that I was to be allowed out, he would come into the room, announcing a uniform inspection or a check of our arms. Then he would say that my pistol was not properly cared for or that there was dust on my shoes. So, after I had gone to the trouble of changing my clothes in preparation for going out, I would be restricted to quarters again.

One day during the dinner hour, this captain decided to ask a question about the phases of the moon.

"Ōsugi!"

I stood when my name was called. Of course, I knew that the moon was in its *kagen* or waning phase that day. But I had never been able to pronounce *k* sounds properly. *T* and *k*—especially *k*—are terrible for anyone who stutters. It is even worse when they are followed by another sound like *ge*, as they were in the word *kagen*. Thus, I had no choice but to say, "It is not in the waxing phase."

"And what phase is it in?"

"It is not in the waxing phase."

"And so what do we call it?"

"It is not in the waxing phase."

"Then, what phase is it in?"

As he continued to press me, it rapidly grew impossible for me to get the words out, so there was nothing else I could do to give a proper military reply except to repeat, "It is not in the waxing phase." Everyone who knew this began to giggle.

"All right! You are restricted to quarters tomorrow!" With that, the captain shouted, " 'tenshun!" and stamped out of the room, leaving us standing there motionless.

I should discuss my stuttering a bit more. My mother blamed it on a rather serious bronchial condition that I suffered when I was young. As I said before, however, many of Father's relatives stuttered and it seems to me that I was born a stutterer. I can remember being almost unable to speak when I was in elementary school, and I have already told how Mother scolded and spanked me when I would stutter. Father was quite worried about my stuttering and whenever he read an advertisement for a medicine or a book labeled, For the correction of speech defects, he would go out to buy and try it out on me. There were never any results.

When I mention this, people laugh. But in fact I have a very shy and self-conscious streak in me. I blush over trifles and get flustered in front of other people. I was probably born this way, yet I think stuttering is partly to blame. When I can't say what it is that I want to say, I get impatient. I become irritated and short-tempered. If anyone should laugh at something, I immediately suspect that they may be laughing at my stuttering and become distrustful. I think that this condition has had a considerable influence on me psychologically.

Let me return to the subject of Captain Kitagawa. One night a fire broke out in the courthouse immediately behind the school. We were awakened by a bugle sounding the alarm for immediate assembly. The office of the registrar and a classroom just over the fence from the court-house had caught fire.

Captain Kitagawa issued a series of orders. The third-year students were assigned to break out the pumps and fight the blaze. The second-year students were sent to patrol here and there. Then he called "Ōsugi!" and the names of one or two of the other four in my five-man squad. He ordered us to take the imperial portrait to the front yard and guard it. Realizing what a great honor this was, we happily dashed off.

After a bit the regimental commander, who rushed to the school when he heard the alarm, came over to the clump of trees where we were standing and started to take a leak. I managed to stammer out in a loud voice, "Commander, sir! The imperial portrait is here!" The officer was very grateful to me and saluted us before he went elsewhere.

We stood the whole night there by the side of the imperial portrait, our mood very serious. By morning I had completely forgotten about Captain Kitagawa's usual hostility toward me.

Later on, after I had been expelled from military cadet school, a fellow named Tanaka was living with me at my lodgings in Tokyo. He was a year older than I and had been expelled from the central military cadet school over some quarrel. Tanaka was from Ise, the same province as Captain Kitagawa, and when Tanaka's old man became worried, he had gone to see the captain. The captain said, "You say he's with Ōsugi? Then you've nothing to worry about." Hearing this, Tanaka's old man was reassured and sent his son the tuition money. When Tanaka showed me the letter from his father, I couldn't figure out what Captain Kitagawa had meant by saying that or what his attitude toward me had been.

The pressure the sergeants were putting on me became more and more severe until once again I came very close to being expelled from school.

In mid-April the entire student body set off on a study tour of the Yamato region. From Nara we made the pilgrimage to Kashiwara Shrine. We climbed Mt. Yoshino in the rain and then stayed the night at some temple. I stayed there with some of the second-year class while the lower classmen stayed in another inn.

When we were on such study tours or at swimming drill, it was almost a nightly occurrence for my "companions" and me to invade the rooms of the left-flank students or the "youngsters" among the lower classmen. That night Sakata and I barged in on the room where a section of the second-year students slept. Along the way I had the feeling that Sergeant Inakuma was watching us through a crack in the sliding doors in the room. But I ignored it, not caring any more what happened.

After some time I saw the doors on the far side of the room slide open a bit and a face like that of the sergeant appeared. Just at that moment I was ——— with one of the youngsters. The sergeant's face withdrew. Sakata, still prowling about the room, hurried out the other door and fled. I simply stayed motionless, looking at where the face had been.

The sergeant returned, bringing the master sergeant with him. They dragged me from the room.

Nothing more came of it that night. The next day we climbed the far side of Mt. Tōnomine and descended to Sakurai at the foot of the mountain. That night I and the right flank of my class were lodged separately in a small inn. At dinner we made a lot of noise and had three servings of rice, but nothing else happened. There was a great deal of discussion of whether I was going to get off without punishment or whether I would get it after we were back at school.

The following day we saw the Kannon goddess of mercy at Hase and then went to the Miwa Shrine. There in the woods behind the shrine, what had to happen finally took place. Colonel Yamada, the school principal, had all the students line up in a semicircle facing me and then he solemnly pronounced sentence on me. The punishment was ten days in the guardhouse and thirty days of confinement to quarters.

VI.

I don't really understand why this discipline had such an effect on me. Yet for the first time in my life—and probably for the last—I felt real

remorse. I spent almost the entire thirty days of confinement in medi-
tation. I resolved to change completely from my former life.

First I stopped smoking. Then I, who had up to then wasted my lei-
sure time running around causing trouble, began to spend a lot of it in
the botanical garden. A gymnasium occupied half the yard in front of
the school, but on the other half was a splendid botanical garden. It had
two greenhouses, one large and one small, and between them stood
what we called the astronomical observatory. Actually it was a building
equipped with a seismograph and fairly elaborate apparatus for mea-
suring such things as temperature, atmospheric pressure, wind velocity,
and rainfall. I doubt that there is a school even today below the level of
third- or fourth-year middle school with such facilities. These facilities
were for the faculty, however, not for students. The instructor of natural history and physical sciences was said to know the principal very
well and had planned these facilities when the school was first built. He
and his young assistant spent all their time in this part of the school, in
the observatory or the botanical gardens or the splendidly equipped science laboratory. They never instructed the pupils on how to use these
things. Eventually, after we left the school, there was criticism from
some quarter and the observatory was sold off to the officer academy or
someplace.

As I walked about the garden reading the small white signs that gave
the Latin and Japanese names for the plants, I constantly mulled over
my life up to that point. This reexamination not only resulted in self-
improvement but also led in another direction. I began to wonder
whether ultimately I could endure military life. I had heard that during
the staff conference at the time of the incident in Yoshino, some officers
had advocated my expulsion. I had been spared because of the efforts of
Captain Yoshida, who was in charge of my section, and Captain Tsuda,
an Aichi man who had replaced Captain Kitagawa. Now I wondered if
indeed it wouldn't have been better if I had been expelled.

The noncommissioned officers, paying no heed to the fact that I had
reformed, continued to trail me like bloodhounds; of course, from time
to time they caught me in some lapse. Above all I wondered if ultimately
I could stand being under the command of such noncommissioned of-

ficers. If they had been commissioned officers, I believed, I could have obeyed and followed their lead. To take orders, however, from these noncommissioned officers, for whom I had neither respect nor affection, was not a question of obedience but of blind submission.

When I considered this question of blind submission, there welled up in me all the grievances and discontent I had felt up to now toward the staff and the upperclassmen. For the first time I thought of Shibata as having a climate of freedom. I recalled how as a mere child I had escaped from the teachers and out from under Father's and Mother's eyes to play all day long on the parade grounds. I longed for freedom.

I think that to a considerable extent I was enticed into this frame of mind by my reading. Reading, other than of textbooks or reference works provided, was strictly forbidden at school. Nevertheless, I often secretly brought in books. I do not recall all the individual names but it was the period in which rising young scholars such as Ōmachi Keigetsu and Shioi Ūkō in Japanese literature and Kubo Tenzui and Kokubu Saitō in Chinese literature were publishing essays in imitation of the classical Japanese and Chinese styles.[17] I became completely engrossed in such reading.

I mention the name Shioi Ūkō here because the only passage from all the works I read at that time that I can still recall is something he wrote: "How fascinating to observe the sight of the flowers of manhood falling in this world." I no longer remember by whom or what or how much I was influenced. Yet I wonder if it wasn't probably the strain of romanticism running through all these works—naive and unsophisticated, yet at the same time free and untrammeled.

It must have been the influence of this reading, but I also wrote some things in imitation of the classical style. My third year had begun. I wrote a piece called "A Visit to the Detached Palace." I remember that my Chinese composition teacher, whose name was Shinomiya Kenshō,

17. Ōmachi Yoshie (1869–1925) and Shioi Masao (1869–1913) were members of the Akamon circle at Tokyo Imperial University and wrote neoclassical poetry as well as elegant prose poems and essays. Kubo Tokuji (1875–1934) was a scholar of classical Chinese, while Kokubu Tanemori (1871–1950) was a historian and magazine editor; both published verse in the classical Chinese style. Here Ōsugi cites their pen names.

critiqued it, saying, "You have not a little talent. Nor is your style without skill. But it is effeminate. This is not the writing of a military officer." When I think back to his remarks, I imagine that I was quite proud of the first part of what he said but annoyed by the last part.

The Japanese composition teacher I had when I was in my second year, whatever his name, lavished much affection on my "talent." One snowy day during the composition period the topic of the day must have been the "elation" of military drill. In explaining this term, he taught us some other phrases. Right away I used one of these other phrases in an essay. A few days later I was called in by the superintendent and asked if I really felt that way. Then he scolded me saying that even if I did really feel that way I shouldn't write such things. Afterward I heard that the teacher was also rebuked for teaching such words.

I visited that teacher's house once or twice. He grumbled on and on about such things as having to eat with the sergeants or master sergeants because of his junior civil service rank.[18] Five or six years later I happened to run into him in the Surugadai district. He spoke with a lonely smile.

"You got out at a good time. I was finally forced to leave too. You wouldn't know of any work I could do, would you?"

That summer when I returned home I carried my report card: it had me first in my class in Instruction (i.e., practical training) with an unprecedented mark of over 19 (20 was perfect); second in my class in Scholastics with a total of 18 point something; and last in my class with another unprecedented score—14 point something—in Deportment. Overall I was 35th or 36th in my class. The melancholia of that youthful return home to Shibata was something I had never known before. And, that melancholia was to grip me for a very long period.

VII.

The night before I left Shibata for Nagoya once again, my father—who had been quietly trying to comfort me all summer with things like a trip

18. The teacher had been appointed as a *hanninkan*—a lower civil-service rank than that of the commissioned officers at the school. I have not been able to reconstruct the meaning of a censored passage: "Sensei wa sō shita *XXXX* shisaya."

to Sado Island—spent the whole evening remonstrating with me for the first time at length about my future. By his side sat my mother, without saying anything, tears filling her large eyes. With that, I pulled myself more or less together and quitted Shibata.

In Tokyo I made a point of picking up bulletins from three middle schools that taught French: the Seijō School, the Gakushūin,[19] and the Gyōsei Middle School. In addition I bought a book called A Students' Guide to Tokyo.

At that time I had not yet actually made up my mind to leave military school. My longing for freedom or whatever was not yet that clearly defined. I was simply so overcome by depression that I could do nothing about it. When I would absentmindedly pick up one of these books, reading it gave me a feeling of soft dreamy contentment.

My depression continued for some time after returning to school. Often I would go into the front yard alone at night to sit on a bench in the botanical garden, crying. Next I would suddenly find myself overcome by spells of vicious feelings. At first I would walk about with an object such as a whip in my hand, bullying second-year classmen and the new admissions. I even became insubordinate to the noncommissioned officers. Then I even failed to salute the officers. Eventually I cut classes and just wandered around school the whole day.

The medical officer diagnosed my case as nervous prostration. I was therefore given a two-week leave of absence. As I passed through the school gates, I resumed my former self. I had a slightly more pensive air about me, yet I was a cheerful youth again. Thus I set off for Osaka.

My uncle was serving as a brigade commander in Osaka. Each day I would take a lunch and a map and roam about Settsu, Kawachi, and Izumi with no particular destination. When I couldn't decide which way to go, I would take out my knife, stand the blade on the road, and go in whatever direction it fell. I returned to school in a fine frame of mind.

Upon my return I immediately fell ill again. I was sick with vicious feelings. It was a madness.

19. In chapter 5 part 1 Ōsugi again refers to this school as the Gakushūin (Peers school). It is distinct from Tōkyō Gakuin in chapter 5 part 2.

During that period a disturbance over some matter broke out between the Aichi men and the Ishikawa men. The Ishikawa men sought help from the power-holders among the students from Tokyo and other prefectures. I had always carried a large knife with me everywhere. Once I even threatened a sergeant who had got too close to me. Everyone knew about it and four or five enemies began to sharpen their own knives. I conferred with four or five allies; then toward evening in front of the fencing hall I challenged one of our opponents—the most powerful of those Tokyo students who had allied against us. As he came toward me, he pulled a knife. The four or five on my side began to back off. I reached in my pocket to draw my knife but changed my mind and instead walked toward him empty-handed. I thought that if I drew the knife that I kept so sharp, I would end by killing him for certain.

As he came on, I seized him by the arm that was brandishing the knife and pulled down and forward. As he went down underneath me, he stabbed wildly and hit me. A sudden chill went through my body. Unable to move my left hand, I stopped grappling with him and got to my feet. He got up too and stood staring at me with a shocked look. Eight or nine students, both friend and foe, gathered around us, all staring at me with shocked faces. As I stood there, blood was turning my body completely red.

"Let's get to the infirmary," I said and headed off. One old orderly was on duty in the infirmary. I stripped in front of everyone and he inspected my wounds. There was one in my neck, another in the left shoulder, and one in the left arm—three altogether. All of them were deep. I asked the orderly, "How about it? Can't you just treat them and keep it among us?"

"Not a chance. These are serious wounds!" The orderly looked at me as if I had said something crazy.

"All right, if there's no other way. Please call the medical officer," I said as I lay down. Then I called the other fellow's name. "We don't have any choice. Let's take the blame, just the two of us."

I saw him nod as I lost consciousness.

When I could get out of bed two weeks later, Father arrived. He had been told about my recent behavior. He requested an honorable discharge from the school, saying, "We can't keep sending a troublemaker like this to school," and took me home with him. After we had been home a bit we received a telegram: "YOUR REQUEST DENIED. ORDERED EXPELLED." The other student was also expelled.

It was the end of November and snow had already begun to fall in Shibata.

A NEW LIFE

1901-1902

I.

After Father brought me home, I was shut up in my sickroom without visitors and left that one room only for daily visits to the neighborhood hospital. The restriction on visitors was something that I had asked for, but Father and Mother interpreted it literally. There were two rooms separate from the rest of the house—a six-mat room and beyond it an eight-mat room. The larger one had been my father's, but he stopped using it entirely. My mother stopped coming to my room almost entirely. The maids and my younger brothers and sisters received strict orders and did not come into this part of the house at all. I later heard that Mother had told them, "Elder brother isn't quite himself, so by no means are you to go in there." Even so, my smallest brother and sister would sneak up as far as the veranda to see what was so strange about me. Then when something happened they would fall over each other as they ran away.

I was being kept out of sight. Yet I did go to the main part of the house to have meals with the rest of the family. Everyone kept silent, staring at my face. I too ate without a word and after eating my meal would return to my room.

In my head were no longer any thoughts about the officers, noncommissioned officers, students—friend or foe—or anything else about military school. Consequently, nothing remained of the vicious moods that had arisen in connection with these things. My life during the two and one-half years at military cadet school—and especially the madness of my life in the last six months—now stood behind me as if merely a vague dream. That dream still depressed me a bit; but in front of me stretched a new, vast, and free world, and my head brimmed with plans for what was to come.

My best subjects in school had been classical and modern languages, and composition. Recently I had completely ignored my studies because I was so engrossed in literature of the romantic style in vogue at the time. Since coming to dislike military life, I often told my friends at school, "You go ahead—become soldiers and head off to war. I'll become a war correspondent and meet you on the battlefield." I didn't necessarily intend to become a journalist. I merely had a vague idea that I would be a man of letters and then, if there was a war, I would become a war correspondent. I thought that I might try writing something like "How fascinating to observe the sight of the flowers of manhood falling in this world."[1]

I would go to senior high school and then to the university. But first of all I would need to be admitted to an advanced class in some middle school and obtain a middle school diploma, I thought. And, having forgotten almost all my English, I would have to choose a middle school somewhere that offered French. The only ones I knew of were the three in Tokyo—Gakushūin, Seijō School, and Gyōsei Middle School.

Spreading out before me the *Students' Guide* I had bought in Tokyo, I learned that numerous schools in Tokyo prepared students for the advanced course in middle school. I knew that my academic skills were not quite up to taking the entrance examination for the fifth-year level of middle school. So, I thought, I should first go to the capital, enter one of those prep schools, and then at the new school year in April take the entrance examinations for a suitable middle school.

Within two or three days after returning home, I decided to do exactly that. Then it was just a matter of watching for an opportunity to discuss the matter with my father. I was confident that a good opportunity would come along soon and that my father would approve;

1. Ōsugi quotes this verse by Shioi Ukō in chapter 4 part 6.

I waited quietly for that time to come. Thus, shut up in the room waiting and dreaming of a free life in Tokyo in the near future, I put aside all my preferences and by myself studied a variety of subjects with all my might.

During this time there was one incident that disturbed my peaceful mood. The family was having more than the usual number of guests and, though my mother tried as far as possible to keep everyone, including herself, from disturbing me, the house was surprisingly busy and noisy. Mother was still treating me very gently and speaking as little as possible; yet I noticed that the solemn dark cast of her face was slowly giving way to a bright happy color. Even from my room I could hear her and the guests chatting gaily and I wondered what it was all about. Then one day I happened to overhear the name Reichan mentioned in the middle of their conversation. Suddenly I had an intuition: Reichan's moving away to become someone's bride.

With that several things flashed through my mind. When our train had stopped at Kashiwazaki on the way to Shibata, I had seen a familiar figure in uniform and full beard standing on the station platform: Reichan's father. My father and he had spoken briefly.

"What happened? You didn't bring her with you?"

"No, we decided to wait a while longer and have Mother and her do it together."

I didn't know what the exchange was about, but when I heard "her" my heart jumped a little. Wrapped in my father's large black cloak over my white hospital gown, I didn't speak as I stole a glance at Reichan's father. The train pulled out with their conversation still bothering me some, but my father and I had come all the way without stopping from Nagoya and had maintained our silence on the train. So I could not ask my father what it had been about.

When we finally arrived home, something else happened. As our carriage stopped at the front door, my mother came rushing out. Looking at our faces, she said disappointedly, "There are just the two of you?" I wondered whom she expected my father to bring with him besides me. It didn't occur to me that there was any connection between this and the conversation at Kashiwazaki.

Now, however, everything was clear. It was obvious that Reichan would soon come here to visit us. And it was obvious that she would be married from here. As I thought this, my heart leapt in my breast. Memories of Reichan—who had been out of my thoughts for so long that I had almost forgotten her—flooded my mind. Feeling that I had to make sure, I went to Mother's room, into the main part of the house for the first time except at meals.

Mother was talking with some women who had come to call. While she talked, she helped the maid and the maid's daughter stuff cotton batting into a quilt with a beautiful pattern that I had never seen before. The maids were chattering.

"A really pretty pattern, isn't it tho'?"

"How nice it'll be to sleep under a quilt as good as this one!"

Entering the room and going up to them, I tried to look as uninterested as possible and asked of no one in particular, "Whose quilt?" I really didn't have the slightest idea what was the topic of their unusually animated conversation, or for what purpose or for whom they were making the quilt.

"You remember the Senda girl, Reichan, don't you, son? Well, the girl is going to be married soon. This quilt, you see, is for Reichan to take along with her. Tomorrow, Reichan and her mother are coming to our house."

When I heard my mother's answer, my face flushed bright red. Trying not to show anyone my red face, I immediately fled back to my room. Once inside, I rested my elbows on the desk and pressed my head tightly between my hands. Closing my eyes, I tried to put out of my mind the brightly colored quilt I had just seen. Hot tears flowed down my face. It isn't enough, I thought, that my family has helped arrange for my sweetheart to marry someone else, but they are so cruel as to make the quilt for the wedding night right in front of my eyes!

Thus in my own mind—though she had been only a childhood friend and I had not given her even a thought for two or three years—Reichan was my sweetheart. Thus I felt now that she was being stolen away from me.

Once Reichan arrived the next day with her mother, however, the joy of living under the same roof with her began to grow considerably stronger than this peculiar feeling of thwarted love.

They were given the room on the other side of the garden, only about four yards away. From my window I could see their faces through the sliding glass doors. Reichan came to visit me in my room almost as soon as they arrived, ignoring whatever my mother must have said to warn them about me, and she continued to come whenever she had free time—or rather, whenever she could escape the watchful eye of her mother.

Never did she show any sign that she was about to be married. Whenever I started to lead the conversation in that direction, immediately—as if to stop my lips—she moved the subject in another direction. Her constant concern was for my injuries, which by now had almost healed. As for my being expelled from school, she actually regarded it as a blessing in terms of my future: "That's fine! Because you'll become a much greater man than you would have as a soldier, you know." I confided in her my plans for the future, and she encouraged me.

"My teachers in school urged even me to go on to normal school and I also wanted to study further but now it's too late. But you, from now you should really study!"

She praised my childhood abilities and shifted to various innocent reminiscences. Almost forgetting that she was soon to be married, I felt a sweetness as if I were talking with a lover as I abandoned myself to reminiscences with her.

One day I heard my mother with Reichan and her mother in their room talking intently in very low tones. I strained my ears to hear.

"What's so strange about him, Auntie? I've gone to his room a lot to chat with him, but I haven't seen a single thing like that. He did tell me he was going to really study from now on and he actually has been studying very hard."

"Well, I wonder. I'd wake up in the middle of the night and hear from that direction the sound of someone turning the pages of a book. And whenever I passed by on the way to the toilet I'd see the light on, but I've just had a sense something might be wrong."

"Yes, he studies until late every night. And he says he wants to go to Tokyo before long to study. And he seems to have already planned everything by himself. Auntie, please—since he's really determined to do

it—I appeal to you and Uncle on Sakae's behalf. You should send Sakae
to Tokyo as he hopes."

"Well, he has been studying so hard, hasn't he. They said he hadn't
quite been himself recently and I didn't know how much to worry. So
I kept quiet and just watched, but there doesn't seem to be any particular thing you could say was strange. Rather you just thought that
something was strange. Reichan, thank you so much. Now I can put my
mind to rest."

Overhearing this, I closed my book and wept silently, alone. I swore
to myself that whatever happened I would study hard and become a
great man, if only for Reichan's sake.

Reichan came to visit me unusually late that evening. When she did
not mention that day's conversation, I could not bring myself to say
anything about it either. But my heart was full of unspoken gratitude
toward her. We sat up through the night talking about childhood memories and, as ever, she consoled and encouraged me before returning to
her room.

The next day, beginning very early in the morning, the house was full
of commotion, and that evening everyone except the maids and children
went out. I thought to myself that Reichan had finally gone to be married. Though I felt very lonely now that she had left without another
word, I no longer had that peculiar feeling that my sweetheart was being
taken from me. I merely wished her happiness and then repeated to myself the vow I had made the previous day.

II.

Four or five days later in the evening my parents called me in. Father's
face no longer showed any trace of the scowl it had worn since he picked
me up in Nagoya. Mother's face had also lost that look, that look as if
she didn't know me, which appeared whenever I entered a room. Now
she greeted me with a smile.

My father's tone was also as warm as he could be, but he only asked
the simple question: "What do you intend to do now?"

I answered clearly but also in simple words what it was that I had
decided on my own.

"It's the literature that bothers me a bit," Father said, frowning and cocking his head to one side after he had heard me out.

"What's this about literature?" my mother asked worriedly, looking at Father's face.

"That's what the Kuwanos' son did."

"Is that the one who graduated from university and doesn't do anything but play about—that one?"

"Um, that's the one. And that's what bothers me, you see."

"Yes, I see."

I didn't know what kind of a fellow this Kuwano was whom they were talking about. But when Mother said that, it seemed that she was going to agree with Father. Then he frowned and cocked his head again.

"In any case, we intend to send you to Tokyo to study, but please try to think again about this thing with literature. You're the first son of all the nine children, you know, and so if you'll study something like medicine or engineering with a sound future, I'll even send you through university. But literature really bothers me."

"Even so," Mother said, "after he's gone ahead and made up his mind, we shouldn't ask him to change it right away. Let's let him think about it for a day or two, alright?" Having said that to Father, she turned to me: "Father has said that we will send you to Tokyo; go back to your room for tonight and think about it some more."

I went back to my room happy with that, believing I had won 70 percent or 80 percent of my goal.

The next day, probably at my father's request, a medical officer who had a university degree came to the house and strongly urged me to become a physician. This was the Dr. Hirano who had been my doctor since childhood and, as I related earlier, had got them to pass me during the physical exam for military school despite my poor eyesight. I didn't have the slightest interest in becoming a physician, however. Nor was I interested later, after I finished at the Foreign Language College, when Dr. Kaji, the present head of the Commoners Hospital, suggested that I go with his son Tokio to France and study medicine. Eventually I did become interested in natural science; even today I wonder if it would have been better if I had studied medicine at that time.

Then the perfect mediator appeared. He was a young first lieutenant named Morioka whom my father thought a great deal of. No doubt Father had discussed me with him. The lieutenant came into my room and counseled me as if we were friends. He discussed matters with me from the standpoint of my family's financial situation and then asked me to reconsider.

"Your father, you know, has said he is really bothered by the literature part—isn't there something else?"

Seeing that university was out of the question, I revealed my alternative plan: "In that case, then I'll go to language school."

The lieutenant gave his hearty approval as soon as I said language school. "That would be fine. Your father would surely approve of that. And if he doesn't approve, leave it to me to get him to approve."

In those days enthusiasm for foreign language study erupted at frequent intervals within the army like a recurrent fever—especially among the military stationed in the countryside. Even if you had never attended the Military Staff College, if you managed to get some language study then you could be posted abroad or in some position of responsibility and thereby have a good chance of advancement. Lt. Morioka, it turned out, came out of the cadet school where he had taken French. I heard that Reichan's husband, a first lieutenant named Sumida, had made a speciality of English at middle school and wanted to go to Tokyo to enter a language school. Even my father had once done some French and then some German, and at that time he was beginning Russian. It is a comment on the times that Lt. Morioka and my father both gave their immediate approval to my second proposal without either one having any idea of what I would do after I finished language school. But I knew full well that as a graduate of a language school I could enter the university in the elective program and later take the examination to transfer into the regular program.

Thus I received permission to go to Tokyo right away. I decided to leave early on the morning of New Year's Day. The carters, however, would not go on New Year's so I had no choice but to wait until the next day, the second.

New Year's began warm and fair but became cloudy about noon and by evening snow was falling thick and fast. That night, a little after midnight, I set off through the three- or four-foot snow on a sleigh pulled by two carters. Mother came out of the house to see me off alone. "Well, you certainly look happy now that you're going," she said, as she wept tears of happiness.

We got as far as the outskirts of town without any trouble, but once outside town the sleigh sank into the snow and would not move another inch. The carters' boss had predicted that this would happen and had wanted us to give up for that night. I wouldn't listen, so finally he had relented and sent the two men with the strongest legs. But the road outside town was buried in snow so deep that their feet sank until snow swallowed them up to the thighs at every step. The sleigh was almost impossible to pull that way. Moreover, the cab on top where I sat was struck again and again by gusts of wind so strong that they threatened to overturn it.

Finally the men halted, saying, "It's useless."

"Then how about going on foot?" I suggested. "One of you lead the way and I'll follow in his footprints. The other can carry my bag and bring up the rear. I could take the lead sometimes or follow behind with my bag."

They were quite pleased with my suggestion. "We promised the boss and his missus we'd make sure we got you there safe and sound, so we don't want to go back either and have to tell 'em we couldn't make it."

They quickly found a place nearby to stash the sleigh and we set off as I had suggested. We had a long way to travel. The nearest train stop was on the Hokuetsu line in Niitsu, almost twenty miles from Shibata. On our way we had to pass through a number of open fields where sometimes there wasn't a house for a mile or even two. The snow continued. It fell unceasingly in fine flakes so thick that we couldn't see a thing beyond a few feet in front of us. The falling snow alone would not have been such a problem, but the wind grew stronger and lifted the snow from the ground to blow it in our faces. When it got that strong we could do nothing but stand still, protecting our faces with our hands, and wait for it to die down. Then we would trudge on, dragging our feet encased in the heavy snow boots up the sloping road, sinking in above our knees at each step.

About halfway between Niitsu and Shibata, on the other side of a town called Suibara, is a plain about two and a half miles wide. As we crossed it all three of us were ready to drop from exhaustion and hunger. I don't know how many times we fell down on that plain. We would take ten steps and rest, then another five steps and rest. By the time we came upon a single house sitting in the middle of the plain, we all were like dead men.

We stopped at the house, throwing ourselves down around the roaring fire in its huge hearth, and slept a full hour. Once we had slept and gulped down seven or eight bowls of hot rice gruel, we felt our spirits revive.

Along about evening we finally managed to arrive in Niitsu before my train was due. After a bit, it too arrived.

As soon as I reached Tokyo I went to Yarai-chō in Ushigome and stopped at Ōkubo's house. His father was a captain who had retired or was just about to. Whenever I was in Tokyo I always visited the Ōkubos and knew there was a lodging house just across the street from them, so I had suggested to my father that I live there and the Ōkubos could watch after me. Fortunately, the lodging house—the Wakamatsuya—had a vacant room of four and a half mats in the rear. I moved in and spent the New Year's vacation searching for a suitable school.

Ultimately I entered what was called the Middle School Fifth-Year Test Course at the Tokyo Gakuin (which no longer exists) in Sarugakuchō and commuted there every day. I focused my energies on the subjects in which I thought I was weak—mathematics, physics, and chemistry. At the same time, starting perhaps in April, I went at night to what was called the French Language School, which had just opened in Tansu-machi in the Yotsuya district. It was headed by a military professor named Shōji (he was the old man of the Shōji whoever recently labeled the "first lieutenant of the workers").[2] He had started it with

2. We may surmise from Ōsugi's tone that this Shōji was not a political ally, but there was a Shōji Hikoo (born 1896) who served as a Socialist member of parliament in the 1950s; George O. Totten lists him as a prewar leader (*The Social Democratic Movement in Prewar Japan*, 422).

another army professor named Andō (who became a professor at Waseda)[3] and a Frenchman named Giraud, a teacher at a higher school.

Thus from the moment I arrived in Tokyo I studied night and day as if in a trance, thinking of nothing else.

But my greatest pleasure came from the freedom that I had for the first time in my life. Living across from me at the lodging house was a captain who was supposed to supervise me as my guarantor, but he was a good-natured old fellow. Never once did he come to spy on me in my room or give me anything resembling instructions. He never even questioned me about what I was doing. I was completely free, acting in whatever way I thought best. I alone had decided to enter the Tokyo Gakuin and the French Language School as well. I simply informed the captain and my father. This was the first time that I determined my actions and life by myself alone, and from then on I followed this practice. Or I should say rather that I grew steadily more and more presumptuous.

At military school I had thought about the free environment of the Shibata I knew as a child, when I used to escape the eyes of my parents and the teachers at school to pass the entire day playing at the parade grounds. Now I had gained that freedom completely. My teachers at the Tokyo Gakuin acted as if they were there simply to teach what had to be taught, unconcerned with whether the students learned or did not learn. It did not seem to matter to them whether you came in or left during the class hour, whether you napped or chatted during the class hour, or even whether you attended. At the French Language School, except for me the students were all adults and the teachers and pupils all interacted as if friends. In contrast to the military school, where we sat for the whole hour without moving our bodies, hands placed just so on our knees, staring unblinking at the teacher's face, this was a completely different world. My responsibility was to myself and myself

3. Andō Takayoshi (1854–1920), reputed to be "one of the two greatest French literature scholars of the day," taught at the Military Staff College and founded the French Literature Department at Waseda University (*Dai jinmei jiten*, 1:131).

only. And I became absorbed solely in the studies for which I was answerable to no one else.

III.

This joyful infatuation with freedom was not simply a vague instinctive goal for me alone; soon the opportunity came for me to link it with theory and extend it to society. The opportunity came quite unexpectedly.

I have already written about one episode from my memories of this period in "From Amidst the Cremated Ashes" in the volume *The Honor of Beggars:*

> It was around May of my eighteenth year (or perhaps two or three months later). I had only recently arrived from the country and was absorbed in preparing for the school entrance examinations. I knew absolutely nothing about world affairs and at that time never gave any thought to such matters. My lodgings were in the Yarai-chō section of Ushigome. There were five or six students from W (Waseda)[4] University and one cold evening they went rushing pell-mell out of the house. I could hear the noise of what seemed a great crowd waiting outside. I opened the sliding window to look out. At least twenty students were there, all wearing the distinctive four-cornered cap with its tassel, milling about boisterously, holding aloft paper lanterns on poles and waving them like huge banners.
>
> "It's getting late! If we don't run all the way, we'll be late!"
>
> "But that's better! It's too cold to walk. Besides, we'll get a lot of attention if so many of us trot through the streets."
>
> "You're right! Let's run! Let's run!"
>
> And they all flew off, shouting loudly to one another in high spirits.
>
> Even now the scene floats clearly in my memory: the flickering lights in the big paper lanterns illuminating the bold letters "Y (YANAKA) VILLAGE COPPER POLLUTION PROBLEM MASS MEETING." And I can still hear their voices chanting "Left, right; left, right" long after they were out of sight.

4. Ōsugi provided the identifications in parentheses: the men were all major figures in the left-wing movement as well as successful journalists and will be identified more fully as they appear in later sections; Waseda was and remains a prestigious private college whose uniform included the four-cornered square cap referred to below; the *Yorozu Chōhō* had one of the largest readerships in Japan with a circulation well over 100,000.

This incident was what first impressed on my mind the name of Y village.[5] From then I began to read with considerable care the Y (Yanaka) village articles that appeared frequently in the one newspaper I was taking at the time—the Y (*Yorozu Chōhō*) *News*.

The Y village problem soon waned. As I think back on it, that was about the end of the great public commotion over it. Accordingly my own interest in the Y village also died out for a time. But thanks to this incident I first learned the names of D (Kōtoku) and S (Sakai) of the Y (*Yorozu Chōhō*) *News*, and K (Kinoshita Shōkō) of the M (*Tōkyō Mainichi Shimbun*) *News* and A (Abe Isoo) of W (Waseda) University. Thus I developed an interest in the numerous social issues appearing at the time in these papers; in particular the writings of S and of D were hugely appealing to me. Later at school in the spring of the following year I wrote essays with titles such as "A Discussion of the Gap between the Rich and the Poor" and began to feel as if I too were a kind of a social revolutionary.

I was not alone. The great majority of the promising young men who flocked to join the new Socialist movement had been led into the movement through the copper pollution issue or through its stimulus had become interested in social problems. This began when D and S left the Y *News* because of their stand against war and started a weekly newspaper (*Heimin Shimbun*).[6]

This is an excerpt from what I wrote about the copper pollution problem at Yanaka village. Though of course there are no falsehoods in it, it errs in tilting a bit too much toward the copper pollution problem. As I reread these lines now in the light of my memories of how I felt about freedom at that time, I need to rectify this tilt somewhat. At least that is my real belief now.

I first took the *Yorozu News* merely because it was the cheapest newspaper. Having just come from the provinces, a world preoccupied with military life, and having for years been forbidden to read newspapers, I did not know its name much less what kind of paper it was.

5. Yanaka was among the villages along the tributaries of the Tonegawa River where the mining operations of the Ashio Copper Company caused flooding and pollution and generated national concern in the 1890s (Fred G. Notehelfer, "Japan's First Pollution Incident").

6. The semifictional piece "From Amidst the Cremated Ashes" (*Shika no naka kara*) was written in collaboration with his second wife, Itō Noe; it appeared in the fall of 1919 and was reprinted in a 1920 collection, *The Honor of Beggars* (*Kojiki no meiyo*). This passage can be found in *Ōsugi Sakae zenshū* 3:548–49.

About the only two national events in those years that I recall anything about were the marriage of the crown prince (the present emperor) and the assassination of Hoshi Tōru. The marriage of the crown prince occurred shortly after I entered cadet school. We were taken to greet the couple at the station precincts as the two passed through on their pilgrimage to Ise Shrine. I recall that we were deeply grateful when they kindly returned our salutes. It is a sidelight, but Yamakawa Hitoshi, who was to become one of my shining mentors, was at that time already publishing a small magazine about Christianity. He made some criticism of the marriage and was sent up for something like three years and nine months on a charge of lèse-majesté.[7]

Hoshi Tōru's assassination took place the year I left cadet school. I heard about it in the schoolyard from a friend who had lived at Hoshi's as a student houseboy. All I felt about it was admiration for the steadiness of hand of the swordsman Iba.[8] I had no idea what kind of man Hoshi was or what he had done wrong.

So by sheer chance it fell to the *Yorozu Chōhō News* to take me by the hand and lead me out of blindness. Through the *Yorozu Chōhō News,* for the first time I was exposed to life as it was lived in the world outside the military. It especially made me see society's unjust and immoral aspects.

To my eyes, however, this injustice and immorality reflected the simple realities of the world. They were purely abstract matters, not subjects that I could say stirred the innermost regions of my heart. Rather what amazed me was the free and untrammeled tone of the whole newspaper. I was especially astonished by the articles signed with the name Shūsui.[9] Nothing frightened him or blocked his way. Brandishing the

7. Yamakawa (1880–1958) was a young Socialist who in 1897 dropped out of the preparatory school for Dōshisha, the Christian school in Kyoto, moved to Tokyo, and for three years lived a student life not unlike Ōsugi's a few years later. In 1900 Yamakawa was charged with lèse-majesté for an article in an obscure monthly that criticized Christians who revered the imperial family.

8. In June 1901 Iba Sōtarō cut down Hoshi, a flamboyant onetime Speaker of the House of Representatives who was involved in bribery scandals.

9. Shūsui was the nom de plume of Kōtoku Denjirō (1871–1911), a pioneer in Japanese anarchism who was executed after being convicted of plotting the death of the emperor. The term was also used of keen-bladed swords, hence the allusions Ōsugi makes in the next paragraph.

pen in his hand exactly as if it were the naked blade his pseudonym implied, he cut his way wherever his beliefs led him. I was absolutely awed by his merciless attacks on militarism and the military. I, born to a military family, raised among military men, given a military education, and then coming to curse the blind obedience and binding fetters of that military life, was enchanted by these qualities of Shūsui's antimilitarism.

It was among Shūsui's circle that I discovered new, and this time true, "companions." However, one thing irritated me. Because I liked the image of a blade flowing like water, I had secretly chosen the nom de plume Shūsui for my own; and now that I learned of a famous man who already had Shūsui as a pen name, I'd have to abandon it.

Someone else with whom I had closer contact also helped open my eyes—a man named Sasaki who had the room next to mine at the lodging house. He was an older student, about thirty, who had graduated from Waseda two or three years earlier. Every year since, he took the higher civil service examination and failed each time. His kimono was dirty and worn and he shaved his head like a Buddhist priest. He would often growl at the maid in his thick Akita accent, his voice loud but affable. In spite of his forbidding mustache, he had a pleasing face, plump with a dimple in both cheeks when he smiled. I had no friends and soon struck up an acquaintance with this veteran student. Sasaki loved to argue, even with a child like me. Not wanting to be defeated, I would let fly with a barrage of things that I had got someplace from reading Shūsui.

Sasaki had a friend named Onodera whom I knew from the French Language School. In the same advanced class as I, Onodera had also graduated from Waseda two or three years before and was now a researcher in sociology under Dr. Tatebe. He was small and, despite protruding front teeth, handsome with the air of a young court noble. One evening we were returning from class with another student named Takahashi, a captain in the transport corps. Takahashi asked Onodera what sort of things one studied in sociology.

Onodera answered proudly. His accent was as thick as Sasaki's but he spoke as if delivering a lecture. "Well, let's consider the state, for example. And below you have the various institutions, you see. In sociology we investigate such things as how these came to be and in what manner they have developed."

"That sounds interesting," Captain Takahashi said, sounding really envious although he was an equestrian instructor at the Army Officer School and was said to be such an accomplished rider that he could control a galloping mount with a single thread for reins.

This was the first I had ever heard of sociology or what it was about. And I joined Captain Takahashi in envying Onodera for doing such scholarship. So I asked Takahashi and Onodera to lend me some books on sociology and on psychology as a fundamental science. I read them intently, even the parts I couldn't understand at all. One work was probably the sociology of Endō Ryūkichi put out by Waseda and another, the sociology of a man named Totoki something, published by the Hakubunkan. I read them through. I also read Kaneko Umaji's history of psychology, entitled something like "Recent Psychology," and an introductory collection of lectures on philosophy also published by Waseda.

In addition, Onodera urged me to read a French edition of Le Bon's *Psychologie des foules,* saying it was a very interesting book. By checking the dictionary over and over again, I finally managed to finish it, though I didn't understand anything.[10]

There were no vacancies that April at the Gakushūin nor was it possible to get into the Gyōsei Middle School. Therefore I went to take the entrance examination at the only school left, the Seijō Middle School. On the application I put down French as my foreign language and the school accepted it. When the day of the examination finally came, however, they told me, "No more French students are being taken into the fifth-year class at this time." Applying there had been a waste of time.

I had no choice except to wait until September and take the English examination at some other middle school. I quickly began to study English. I had heard that you could pass the test at any school if you could read English at the level of the fourth book of the *Union Reader* series.

10. A decade later, in 1914, Ōsugi published his translations of Le Bon's works, *La Naissance et l'évanouissement de la matière* and *Les Idées nouvelles sur la matière.*

Therefore, stopping my other studies, I started going to an English teacher in the neighborhood for lessons on the fourth book of that series. Since I hadn't glanced at an English text for several years, I was rather rash to start on the fourth book. Nevertheless, I studied with all my might, going to hear the teacher's lectures and then returning to my room to read with a dictionary and a guide for self-study. After a month or two the fourth book of the *Union Reader* ceased to cause me great problems.

Then, without warning, one day in July or August I received a telegram from my father: "MOTHER IN CRITICAL CONDITION — COME AT ONCE."

CHAPTER 6

MEMORIES
OF MOTHER
1902-1904

I.

My family had moved into a house just by the entrance to the parade grounds in Nishi-ga-wa, which was the neighborhood next to Onoechō. I was very familiar with the house. A Major Tanioka had lived there, and his son and I had been in the same class in middle school. Tanioka failed the entrance examinations for both the Army Officers School and the cadet school. Giving up the idea of being a soldier, he entered Keiō[1] and I hear that now he is a financial reporter for some newspaper. First Lieutenant Matsushita Yoshio, who later was expelled from school for embracing Socialist ideas, lived in the house behind ours. At that time, of course, he was still a young boy and a friend of my younger brother.

When I entered the front door, I saw a crowd of people, some I knew and some I didn't, milling around weeping. I thought to myself, Mother's dead; she's just died. Stopping someone, I demanded, "Where's my mother?" The woman stared at me wide-eyed for a moment, crying, then without answering she moved away as if to avoid me. I stopped another woman. Again I got the same response.

Giving up and thinking that my mother was probably in an inner room, I followed the first woman into the room directly off the

1. This well known private school in Tokyo was especially noted for its courses in political economics and commerce.

vestibule. The door between that room and the adjoining sitting room had been left open and the two rooms were filled with seated people. As I entered they all turned and stared at me just as the other two had, their eyes swollen from weeping. "Where's my mother?" I demanded again, and the women broke into loud sobs. No one among them would answer me. I began to feel uneasy and, not knowing what else to do, went back to the vestibule and opened the door into the room beyond. This, I could see, was my mother's room. Her chest of drawers and dressing table were against one wall. But no one was in the room. I stood there in a daze, wondering what could have happened.

At that point another woman came in. I've forgotten her name but she was an army wife who was a close friend of my mother and also a person of whom I was fond. Like the rest, she had eyes swollen from crying but spoke as if scolding me.

"What's happened with you? Did you come ahead?"

I didn't understand what she meant by "ahead" but answered, "No. I've just come from Tokyo."

"Then you didn't go to Niigata?"

"No, I didn't. Is my mother in Niigata?"

"Well, then you haven't heard anything? Oh! . . . ," she responded, tears streaming down her face.

"Is Mother dead?"

"Yes. She passed away yesterday at the Niigata Hospital. Your family is supposed to be back here very soon."

Hearing this, I suddenly realized—of course, none of my family were at home. At the same moment I thought about the telegram. It was the first one I had ever received. Inside I had read, "MOTHER IN CRITICAL CONDITION—COME AT ONCE" and hadn't looked to see where the sender was. Shocked, I had rushed to borrow train fare from the Ōkubos across the way and then straight to Ueno Station.

"They're here!" someone called from the other room, and I could hear everyone going to the front door to meet them. The woman brought me out of my daze, saying, "Well, it seems they're back." She started out of the room. I followed behind her. Outside, having just got out of the carriage, stood Father, four or five friends, and the children, all around the coffin.

Later I was told that when I arrived people thought that the whole family had come and came to the front door to greet them. When I entered alone and wandered about asking, "Where's my mother?" they all thought that I had gone out of my mind.

My mother had died of an abscessed ovary, or what is commonly known as abdominal dropsy. Shortly before, in poor health ever since giving birth to her ninth child, she had gone off to spend some time at a hot springs. Right after returning home she had gone to Niigata, explaining that she was going to have surgery. She left in good spirits, saying, "Why, in two weeks I'll be back as good as new again."

"That was the way your mother was. What's more, she said that since Sakae is busy studying for his examinations, we mustn't worry him; and she absolutely refused to let anyone tell you."

The night Mother's body came home I kept the vigil with a woman named Okaka who lived in San-no-chō. She had been my mother's hairdresser from the very first day we moved to Shibata. She was more than her hairdresser, having become her very closest confidante. While we sat up she told me the story. And last summer when I secretly visited Shibata after a twenty-year absence in order to prepare this autobiography, the old granny who had once been Okaka was the first person I went to visit.

"It couldn't have been more than three or four days after that, when you received that telegram saying she was dangerously ill. I took all the children along with me to visit, but by then she was already in great pain, don't you know. Giving her shots they managed to keep her living from one hour to the next. Often she would ask, 'Isn't Sakae here yet?' And because the pain was too much even for a strong person such as herself, she would ask us over and over to let her die. Then I would tell her Sakae is on his way and she would nod her head at me and fall quiet. She nodded to say that whatever happened, she was going to wait for you. Again and again she would ask to die quickly, but each time, when I mentioned you she'd nod and become calm."

All night long Okaka just went on repeating this story to me—she was crying and I was crying too. Okaka told me something else as well.

"When your mother left she said to me in a loud voice, 'Okaka, I'll soon be well again and come home.' But actually she had already resigned herself. When I went to the house to get the children, to take them with me to see her, I opened the drawers where your mother kept her clothes. Each thing had a curious card pinned to it. When I looked closer, I saw that each card had one of the girls' names—Haru, or Kiku, or Matsue—written on it. It made me angry, don't you know. I thought to myself that if she'd already made up her mind she was going to die, wouldn't it be better not to have bothered to go all the way to Niigata for an operation? I reproached your mother about it—speaking my mind, I did." Okaka went on to say that my mother's death was actually the doctor's fault. She told me about how Mother had pains in the abdomen after surgery; when they cut her open again they found that the stitches had come loose inside and there was a terrible abscess. Everyone was outraged and said that the matter should be taken up with the hospital. Father alone was resigned, his face full of sorrow. "No—what's finished is finished."

The vigil lasted two or three nights. Then, when my grandmother (Mother's mother) arrived from Osaka and my older sister Haru got there, we held the funeral.

I was given a memorial tablet to carry. The procession moved slowly through the busiest street in Shibata—the one that ran from one edge of town almost to the other—until we reached the Bodaiji, the family temple of the former lord of Shibata. Whenever my mother went out during the more than ten years we lived in Shibata she greeted almost everyone she met on the street, speaking the local dialect in her loud voice. Now, not only had large numbers of people come to pay their respects at the funeral but also as we passed through the streets almost all the residents came outdoors to pay their respects. Okaka of San-no-chō still boasts, rocking her uncommonly small body back and forth and wrinkling up her plump face, "I've yet to see a more splendid funeral."

After the ceremony was over, six bearers lifted Mother's coffin and on foot, with my younger brother Nobu alongside, we took it to the cremation site in the hills near Ijimino where I had so often gone to play. There the bearers spread a layer of straw on the ground and gathered pine boughs to pile onto the straw. Then they placed the coffin and put more boughs on top. This done they spread mats in a circle about six yards away and unpacked boxes of food and several jugs of sake. They would sit there and drink until morning, they said, waiting for the body to be reduced to bones and ashes.

Following their directions, I lit a sheaf of straw and set fire to the bottom layer of straw under the coffin. It burst into flames. The fire soon spread to the pine needles and boughs above. Within those blazing flames I again saw Mother's face, still full and round but much discolored from being made to wait days in the summer heat, as she lay on her side as if asleep in the coffin. It would be unbearable, I thought, if her face, or hand, or foot, should appear as the coffin burned away. Nonetheless I remained staring into the fire.

Then a bearer suddenly drew my brother and me aside and urged us to return home now. It was almost dark and we had been told before coming that we were not to stay too long. The man led us to the foot of the hill and from there we rode home in a carriage.

II.

I had not given Reichan a thought in some time until the day they brought home my mother's body and I saw Reichan standing next to the coffin. She had been with my mother in Niigata during the last few days. That same night, I think it was, she had been persuaded to go home quite late only after everyone said several times that it was senseless for her to keep vigil with the body. One of the women touched me on the shoulder like a conspirator and suggested in a loud voice that I see Reichan home. She was, next to Reichan, the prettiest wife in the regiment: young and married to the first lieutenant who served as a brigade adjutant under my father, the superior adjutant. I had been friendly with her from before. Others joined in urging me to go ahead. I wavered, my heart pounding. Reichan smiled hesitantly and seemed to wait for me to stand up. The other attractive young wife also smiled and watched my face. The smiles of these two lovely young wives stirred me peculiarly.

I quickly got a lantern and left with Reichan. Outside was pitch-dark. Our bodies were so close that they almost touched as we started off. It was the first time I had ever walked so close to her. I forgot everything else, even my mother's death. As we walked on by the dim light of the lantern we drew even closer. Walking like that, we talked loudly and laughed gaily.

"Oh! Isn't that you, Saitō?" Reichan exclaimed.

Suddenly a man in uniform came toward us at a vigorous pace. As we were about to collide with him, Reichan recognized him as Lt. Saitō, one of her husband's fellow officers. I also knew Lt. Saitō when he was still a probational officer before I entered military school, but he didn't seem to recognize us now.

"Who're you!" he shouted, looking as if he would spring at Reichan.

"Hold it! It's me," I said, stepping forward and shielding Reichan. "It's me."

The lieutenant peered into my face for a moment. "Oh, it's you. I'm sorry. I . . . I was just on my way to your house. Please excuse me." His words were more friendly, but as he left he still looked angry.

After we had gone a ways, Reichan looked back over her shoulder and muttered, "Really! That Saitō is disgusting. And he reeked of alcohol."

"Still, we were laughing a lot, and in this neighborhood he may have misunderstood." Both Nishi-ga-wa, the street we were on, as well as Okohitomachi, the next one over, were full of brothels patronized by soldiers.

"Well, that's true. But even so, he was very rude!" She was still somewhat indignant but at the same time a little self-conscious.

Neither of us spoke for a while but we went on walking as close together as before, our bodies almost touching.

"You know, Sakae, being married has been awfully hard on me." Reichan broke the silence in a soft voice.

"How so?"

"Father-in-law, he's mean. Mother has been all right so far, but that father—he's been the difficult one. He finds fault with everything, even the way I use chopsticks. Even that wouldn't be so bad, but as soon as I'm out of the house he ransacks my sewing box looking for things. That's really hard to put up with."

"Huh? He does things like that?" I looked at her in surprise. She remained silent, her eyes downcast. Not knowing what else to say, I remained silent also.

We were walking alongside the river where there were few houses and the street seemed lonely. Still very close together, we continued on without speaking until again Reichan broke the silence and asked me about school in Tokyo. I recalled the secret resolution I had made at the end of last year when I promised to become a great man if only for her sake. Yet the thought never occurred to me to mention it to her. Even if I had wanted to talk about it I couldn't have done so. So I just gave answers to her questions until, finally, we arrived in front of her house.

I started to leave, but she urged me to come in for a while. Without thinking, I answered jokingly, "No, your husband is liable to think it strange the way Saitō just did."

"Oh, you're terrible, Sakae. All right, goodnight!"

She glared at me with her hand raised as if she would hit me, then hurried into the house.

I returned home in somewhat of a daze.

The next day Reichan came to the house again. She never missed a day while my mother's body remained in the house, and whenever we exchanged glances we completely ignored what had occurred the other evening. As my mother's many friends did, in fact we mourned Mother's death with heavy hearts; yet from the day after the funeral, whenever we were together, it was enough to make us both forget the death. We felt just like children again, chatting and laughing as merrily as we had when we set out that night.

The other pretty wife also came to visit almost every day. Smiling, she would sit with us just listening and watching our expressions. Sometimes she would tease us about what a happy pair we were. My grandmother kept scowling, as if disgusted.

Later I heard that this other pretty wife had been divorced because something improper took place while her husband was away in the Russo-Japanese War. Not long after I heard that, I caught a glimpse of a woman in the Ginza district and was certain it was she. I wonder where she is and what she is doing now.

With the entrance examinations close at hand, I couldn't remain this way in Shibata forever. A week after the funeral I returned to Tokyo.

There I began to study once again, forgetting all about Mother, Reichan, and the other young wife.

III.

The first of October came and I took the entrance examinations of the fifth year at both the Junten Middle School and the Tokyo Middle School (which no longer exists).

I don't know how matters are arranged now, but in that period almost all the private middle schools in Tokyo held entrance examinations for every grade in each school term of the year. Thus their practice was to gather applicants two or three times at the beginning of each term, give them entrance examinations, and collect the examination fees each time. This was the third and last time of the year for both Junten and Tokyo Middle School to take applicants.

Somehow, I thought, I had to enter the one or the other. But the two tests were to be held at almost the same time. I had sufficient confidence in my scholastic abilities, but in order not to run the slightest risk I decided to have someone take the test at the Junten Middle School for me while I took the slightly earlier one at the Tokyo Middle School. Fortunately, I had just the right person. He was a friend of the boy whose family ran my lodging house, a graduate of Waseda Middle School whom I also knew well.

I hated mechanical drawing and there were three problems in it on the test I took at the Tokyo Middle School. Unable to understand them, I failed the test. My stand-in, however, did quite well, answered every question, and passed. So, thanks to him, I entered the fifth-year class at Junten Middle School.

Before I continue in chronological sequence as I have done, I am anxious to tell the rest of the story of Reichan all at once. I feel rather ashamed to go on telling the story of a first love—a love that has a sweetness even more intense than honey—in bits and pieces. So I want to skip ahead of myself a little to recount all at once the whole story of what passed between us from this point on. Since it includes scenes of my relationship with Reichan that took place around the death of her husband, Sumida, and I think that these contrast with the previous episodes, I want all the more to write them down now.

I had an opportunity to see Reichan on three occasions after the previous episode. The first was hardly worth mentioning. It was some four years later. I had thrown myself completely into the Socialist movement after graduating from the Foreign Language College.[2] Sakai, Tagawa Daikichirō, the late Yamaji Aizan, and others—that is, the social democrats and the state socialists of that time—had united to form a movement against the increase in streetcar fares. They held a citizens' rally at Hibiya and afterward used the crowd to storm the municipal hall and the offices of the streetcar company.[3] It was the day before that. At Sakai's home I picked up some handbills for the next day's rally and started to distribute them in the district around Kōjimachi San-chōme. It was then that I caught a glimpse from across the street of a woman who looked like Reichan. That was all.

Afterward I heard that it had actually been Reichan. Then right after I was arrested at the citizens' rally and was in jail pending trial for the fearful crime called seditious rioting, Reichan went to the place where I had been staying. It was in Shimo-Rokubanchō, where I had been living with a woman some twenty years my senior.

The second occasion that I was to see Reichan—I think two or three years had passed—was when I visited her and her husband, Sumida, at the Tokyo Eisei Hospital. I've forgotten why Sumida was in the hospital or how I knew that she would be there with him. As I entered his room, Reichan ran out without a word and disappeared. Sumida, who was having his back massaged, laughed, "Oh, it's you! Reichan ran out

2. In March 1906 Ōsugi graduated from the French department of the Tokyo Foreign Language College (Tōkyō Gaikokugo Gakkō), not to be confused with the French Language School (Furansugo Gakkō), which he attended before his mother's death.

3. In March 1906 the newly formed Japanese Socialist party (Nihon Shakaitō) joined forces with other groups to campaign against a proposed fare increase on the Tokyo streetcars. The mass rally mentioned here took place on 15 March at Hibiya Park opposite the Imperial Palace, where (according to one source) 10,000 gathered to hear speeches. The crowd then marched through the streets, waving large red flags with the words "Anarchism" and "Communism," obstructing traffic, and breaking windows, thus giving the police the excuse they wanted to arrest radicals. Ōsugi was sentenced to two years but, since it was his first offense, was released on probation after three months; on Sakai Toshihiko, see chapter 1 notes 1, 2.

thinking it was some visitor she didn't know." He sent the masseur to call her back. She came in with a very surprised look on her face.

Sumida told me that he had come to Tokyo and joined the military police because he had wanted to study English. He had been sent to some school for military police and was then transferred out of Tokyo. Now he had returned because of his illness. We talked about my having become a Socialist and having been arrested several times. He said it distressed him but since it was part of my personality there was nothing anyone could do. "Yes," Reichan rose to my defense; "it's because he's too able."

I stayed only about thirty minutes. After that meeting I lost track of them for quite some time. Another four or five years passed, and just as I was becoming involved in those complicated love affairs with Kami-chika and Itō,[4] Reichan suddenly reappeared for the third and last time.

I was leading a French conversation group at the Geijutsu Club in Ushigome. One day when I went there and opened the door to the room I was using, I found Reichan sitting all alone on one of the benches. I was very surprised.

"Sumida's lungs have gotten terribly bad, you see, so he had to give up his command of the military police detachment in Kumamoto to come back here. Since then he's been bedridden, and he's heard that your lungs used to be terribly bad too but that now you're cured. He's been saying he'd like very much to see you and talk about your lungs. The doctors keep saying all kinds of things but I don't understand any of it. He's been sick for a long time and just keeps getting weaker and weaker."

She talked on in great detail until it was almost time for my French group to start and several of my pupils had come in. So I said, "Well, in

4. The public scandal and sensational court trial in 1916 ensured that Ōsugi's readers would recognize the references to Kamichika Ichiko (1888–1981) and Itō Noe (1895–1923). Both women were prominent in their own right: Kamichika as a journalist who helped found the Bluestocking Society (Seitōsha) for women's rights in 1912; Itō as editor of its magazine, *Bluestocking*, in 1915–1916. Ōsugi was married to Hori Yasuko when he began simultaneous affairs with Kamichika and Itō. In 1916 Kamichika attacked him with a knife and spent two years in prison for the assault. Over the next six decades Kamichika continued working for feminist causes and was a prominent Socialist member of the House of Representatives in the 1950s and 1960s. Hori divorced Ōsugi and Itō became his second wife; she died with him in 1923.

that case, I'll come to your house tomorrow," and accompanied her to the front door.

When I went there the next day I could see that Sumida was even worse than I had been told. I had seen several men die of consumption and Sumida had all the symptoms of one who didn't have much longer to live. I thought he couldn't last more than another month. He asked many questions about my condition when I had been bad and the treatment I had received. I answered him in detail. I also encouraged him, saying that he'd be all right. While we talked his coughing became more and more severe, so I turned aside their invitation to stay, thinking it best if I didn't remain any longer. At the appropriate opportunity I took my leave, but only after telling Reichan in private what I had concluded.

I intended after that to visit Sumida frequently but, because I was so busy traveling back and forth hundreds of miles to Onjuku where Itō was staying, I had no free time. While I was still thus tied up, I received word from Reichan that Sumida had died.

I rushed to their house as soon as I heard. There was a large group of men and women around Sumida's body, all of them as if entranced, handing around a large piece of rope that seemed to be a huge rosary and chanting the name of Amida Buddha. Since all the downstairs rooms were crowded with people, Reichan led me directly to the second floor. To this day I never know what to say in the way of condolences to the family of someone recently dead, so I simply bowed silently.

"Well, it was just as you said it would be," she began, her face weary and tear-stained but her voice as animated as ever. "I suppose I shouldn't say this, but I've been resigned to his dying for a long time, and now I feel more worry about what's going to happen to me than grief over his death."

This was unexpected, coming as it did as soon as I arrived.

"I'm not worried financially. I can manage somehow. But with Sumida dead, his relatives have come from all over and I've been going through torture. And they'll go on tormenting me the rest of my life."

Thinking more and more how unexpected this was, I just listened to her go on without making a response.

"As soon as his people get here from his home, they'll ask me why is it I haven't cut my hair yet. People here are already saying that and there's nothing I can answer. Then they'll see the violin hanging on the wall and someone will take it down saying that a widow has absolutely no need for any instruments. I don't care a bit about such things as cutting my hair; I don't want the violin. But when I ask myself if I could suffer living like a nun the rest of my life—that's what they're after— even I get frightened. I've known a lot of army wives, especially during the Russo-Japanese War, who lost their husbands at the front and immediately cut off their hair. I also know well what happened to them after four or five years. Almost none of them remained respectable widows and that's really crueler than living the life of a nun."

It surprised me that Reichan, whom I had thought of as the typical army wife, could see so clearly through the so-called life of the widow. "Then you mean there's no way you could suffer through that?" I asked, trying to find out just how far her resolve went.

"No, I intend to try to suffer through it. Every day they've all been pressing me to go back to Sumida's village and live like a nun, cutting myself off from the world to raise our one child and look after Sumida's ancestral tablets. Well, I'm going to try. I don't know how far I can suffer through it; but whatever happens I'll go on suffering through as long as I can."

"But you're afraid at some point you won't be able to suffer through it, aren't you. What are you going to do then?"

"Yes. That's what worries me. That's what frightens me. But I'll suffer through whatever happens."

"But what do your own father and mother say?"

"They say they're sorry, they're sorry for me. But once having entered the Sumida family I must do as they say."

"If you're really this determined, then it'll be all right. But after all, it's best as far as possible not to suffer. You should never try to suffer through something once you feel it's going to be utterly impossible no matter how hard you try. That's the worst cause of degradation."

"Then what should I do at the point where I can no longer suffer through?"

"There's absolutely no rationale to your suffering through it. No. In a case like this, cast everything aside and fly away. Flee Tokyo immediately. As long as I'm here, I'll see that you prevail whatever happens."

"Thank you so much, Sakae. I think of you as my one and only real older brother. But I'll suffer through with it, all the way through. And please don't ever forget, Sakae, I really do think of you as my one and only older brother."

I almost took her by the hand but instead departed for a pressing appointment I had promised to keep.

Sumida's funeral was held the next day. I didn't have any formal Japanese dress or kimono to wear and there was nowhere I could borrow one, so I deliberately used these circumstances as an excuse and enjoyed spending the day at Kamichika's place in nearby Azabu.

Several days later, Reichan visited me at my lodgings in Kōjimachi. She said she was going to Sumida's home the following day or the one after that. Because she was on her way to visit a relative who lived nearby in Ushigome, it was fortunately possible to stop to see me in secret. Except to repeat in a bit more detail what we had said at her house, there wasn't much more to say. But several times as we talked I had an impulse to take her hand. She had no excuse to prolong her stay, and I also couldn't remain long as it was time for me to leave for the Geijutsu Club. We left my place and went as far as the club building together. There without further ado we wished each other good luck and parted.

IV.

Though no doubt there were many other places like it, the Junten Middle School seemed a strange place. The lower the grade, the fewer the pupils. The fifth-year class in which I was enrolled was divided into three sections with a total of two hundred to two hundred fifty students. The fourth-year class had one hundred fifty in two sections; the third-year, a hundred students and the second-year had only forty-five. No one entered the first- or second-year classes intentionally and the majority entered at the fourth- or fifth-year levels. My fifth-year section included people who had already graduated from such schools as

Waseda and Tetsugakuin (the precursor to Tōyō College) and many other specialist schools. They had come here because a middle school diploma was required for some other things.

Some were youths with the faces of prodigies, others older with blank stares; some were self-educated. There were also quite a few hooligans like me who had been expelled from other schools. Many of them had also used stand-ins to pass the entrance examinations.

A friend named Tosaka entered the school along with me. He had been thrown out of the military cadet school in Sendai for some homosexual misconduct about the same time that I had been expelled from the school in Nagoya. I had met him in January of that year—that is, just after I arrived in Tokyo—in the reception room of the cadet school in Ichigaya. He told me that an old friend of mine from Shibata named Tani had entered military school the same term as he had, and that they and yet another fellow had all been expelled together. The four of us quickly became friends. Somewhere we happened to meet a certain Shimada, who too had been expelled from the cadet school in Osaka about the same time for the same reason, and he too became our friend. The locations were different—Nagoya, Sendai, and Osaka—but all five of us had been at military school and all were in the same grade.

We got together and admonished one another, swearing that we would study hard until we redeemed our honor. Thus, in October we all entered the fifth-year class of middle school.

Among us all, Tosaka and I were the closest, either because of how we met or because we both liked literature and often discussed the relative merits of writers such as Kōyō and Rohan.[5] Right after we entered Junten Middle School we rented a room and lived together in the Ikizaka-shita district of Hongō. While we studied hard in school, we both also read a great many novels. There was a fairly good rental library up the hill from our place from which we borrowed books. Before long we had read almost its entire collection.

5. Ozaki Kōyō (1867–1903) and Kōda Rohan (1867–1947) were two leading writers of the period.

After a while, our friend Shimada came to the lodging house. He was a well-built fellow with a swarthy complexion, quite vain about his skills in fencing; he thought our constant reading of novels was disgusting. So Tosaka and I decided on a plan. We borrowed a copy of the novel *Hotogisu* and forced him to read it against his will.[6] In the beginning he leafed through it looking as if he found it difficult going; but gradually the scowl faded and at the end he was using his ham fists to wipe the tears from his eyes. Tosaka and I, saying "You see," chose something else we thought he would enjoy and presented it to him. But Shimada was entirely taken with Namiroku's novel *Five Men;*[7] he delighted in saying things such as "I'm Kuroda; and you, Ōsugi, you're like Kura-what's-his-name."

Tosaka and I had long since graduated from the sort of things that Namiroku and Gensai wrote; we were even growing dissatisfied with Kōyō and Rohan. So we didn't bother to discuss it with Shimada. Secretly, however, being identified with the character Kurahashi bothered me: Yes, it's true that one side of me is now like Kura-what's-his-name, struggling along, serious and steady-going. But another side of me is like Kuroda, secretly burning with virility. So what good is this pseudovirility of yours going to do you, Shimada? I exclaimed this only to myself. To say, Now, you'll see, gave me strength in my belly.

About that time a student named Tanaka from Nagoya moved into our lodging house. He was a term ahead of us and had been thrown out of the Central Military Cadet School. Then two more came to live there—one a friend of Tosaka and the other of Shimada. These two, however, couldn't stand the dull serious life we led and soon went elsewhere. Another student, also a term ahead of us in school, often visited us as well. His name was Hakoda and he had left his school in Sendai

---

6. *Hotogisu,* the name of a bird and of a very successful novel by Tokutomi Roka (1868–1927) published serially in 1898–1899, was the tragic love story of a naval officer and his young tubercular wife, the divorce forced upon them by his family, and her death.

7. *Tōsei no gonin no otoko* (Five men of the contemporary world) by Murakami Namiroku (1865–1944), a popular work of the day, related the lives and adventures of five students: Kurahashi takes a job to help support them all; he gives Kuroda a share of the first month's earnings, which Kuroda squanders on drink, presumably demonstrating his devil-may-care attitude.

the year before we had; now he was in higher secondary school. Two or three others a term or so behind us also came to hold discussions about school and a variety of matters.

Thus it seemed that our lodging house had become the central gathering place for almost all the "refugees" from military school. The following year we all finished middle school without incident. Shimada and I entered the Foreign Language College; Tosaka and Tanaka went to study at a fisheries institute, while Tani entered a merchant marine school. All of them have done rather well.

Tani is probably the captain of a N.Y.K. Line ship by now. I've heard that Tanaka became an engineer and works for some prefecture. Quite a while ago I learned that Shimada was teaching German in a regimental officers' mess in some rural area. Tosaka, they say, made a great deal of money in fisheries, becoming a man of such means that he once kept two local geisha in the San-in region. But about ten years ago he went bankrupt and moved to America. Even now, it seems, he is in difficult straits. Hakoda is serving as a public procurator or something in Korea.

In addition to the rental library in Ikizakaya-ue, there was another one in the vicinity of Jimbō-chō that was a favorite of mine. Besides novels, it had books on many different difficult subjects. When I was living in a place in Yarai-chō, I started going there, browsing through the books and borrowing ones on philosophy, religion, and social problems. There were two books that I read over and over: *The New Society* by Yano Ryūkei, which I read while living in Yarai-chō, and Dr. Oka's *Lectures on the Theory of Evolution,* which I read while at Ikizaka-shita.[8]

I have no memory of what impressions *The New Society* made on me—possibly because I read it too early. But I can still feel the great

8. *Shinshakai* by Yano Fumio (1850–1931) was a widely read account of a socialist utopia published in 1902; Yano's earlier novel *Keikoku Bidan* (Tales of statesmanship) was said to have inspired at least two of Ōsugi's seniors in the socialist movement, Katayama Sen (1860–1933) and Yamakawa Hitoshi. Oka Asajirō (1868–1914), a Tokyo Imperial University graduate who taught biology at Tokyo Higher Normal School, wrote several popular accounts of evolutionary theory, of which *Shinkanron kōwa* was the best known.

excitement I felt while reading Professor Oka's *Lectures on the Theory of Evolution*. I seemed to be growing taller as the horizon steadily receded. The world, which until then was entirely unknown to me, was opening up before my eyes with each new page. I was too excited to enjoy Oka's book alone and I urged, almost forced, all my friends to read it. The work awakened in me for the first time an interest in natural science. At the same time, this theory of the change and evolution of all things, calling as it did for reforms in the social system that still had great authority in my mind, made it exceptionally easy for me to join the ranks of those advocating socialism: "There is no single thing that does not undergo change. The old collapses and the new rises up. Who is prospering now? Is it not true that soon they will end buried in the cemetery?"

Yet something was still missing from my life. My mother's dying— that I had almost managed to forget, though doubtless there lingered in my mind an unconscious loneliness for her. And Reichan—I had nearly succeeded in forgetting her the same way. Moreover, having completely abandoned homosexual "love" after many years, I felt lonely in that area as well. For friends I had only my band of warriors dropped from cadet school. To the extent that we were all struggling in the same circumstances, we did not really have relationships in which we could be unreservedly intimate.

Probably in an effort to satisfy this hunger, I often went to visit my relatives in Iigura. It was the home of the wife of my cousin, Yamada Ryōnosuke (now a major general and commander of a military police unit). Yamada was then a student at the Military Staff College and lived in a small house in Iigura. I wanted to immerse myself in the intimacy of such relatives as these. I also wanted to soak in the agreeably luxurious life of their mansion. And I wanted to see the smiling faces of the various pretty girls there.

While everyone in the family, male as well as female, was quite good looking, the faces and hearts were cold. I felt this even more once I had been thrown out of military school. One of the girls, two or three years younger than I, had often passed the time and joked with me when I was in cadet school. I even had a secret wish in my heart: if only I already had my commission . . . Now she was very ladylike and just put on airs around me.

Not long before I graduated from Junten Middle School, I began to visit Christian churches here and there. It was chiefly this loneliness that led me to do so, but the need for new and progressive ideas also contributed. I ended up attending the Hongō church of Ebina Danjō.[9] It was not only the one closest to my lodgings but I liked his sermons best. I do not know whether I was unaware of Ebina's nationalism or whether perhaps it suited the military spirit lingering still in the back of my mind. In any case, I was completely entranced by the preacher's eloquence. His wonderful voice enthralled me whenever, pushing back his grey hair and stroking his long beard, he would thrust up his hands and raise the pitch of his voice, invoking God. And when his voice choked with tears, I joined the other believers in weeping.

The reverend often urged that we receive baptism, saying, "No, it does not matter if you do not yet understand Christianity well—No sooner will you receive baptism than you will immediately understand it well." For a rather long time I hesitated, but finally I was baptized. Thinking that I would be soaked, I had my hair cropped close before receiving the cup of water.

Christianity had considerable influence on me insofar as it encouraged the "serious and steady-going" side of my personality. But the influence did not last long.

V.

Immediately after I passed the entrance examinations for the Foreign Language College, I went to visit my father in Fukushima. Shortly before he had taken the blame for some misconduct by the officer whom he was serving as adjutant and had been transferred from his post as brigade major, relegated to that of regimental adjutant in Fukushima.

9. Ebina Danjō (1856–1937), pastor of this Japanese Congregational church in the Hongō district of Tokyo between 1897 and 1920, was one of the most influential Christian intellectuals of his day. Although Ebina's nationalism is stressed here, the Hongō church attracted social democrats and moderate reformers who eventually opposed non-Christian radicals like Ōsugi—see part 5 below.

Afterward Father's elder brother told me the story. Father had argued with the division commander. Father's brigade commander, Hishijima Yoshiteru, had not got along with their division commander —or I should say, the division commander hated Hishijima. As Hishijima's adjutant, Father had to take the side of the brigade commander. Once before Hishijima had been retired because of financial debts. During the Sino-Japanese War he had been reactivated, only to find himself once again deeply in debt. My father, while officially serving as Hishijima's adjutant, was in fact kept busy attempting to put Hishijima's personal finances in order. Several times Hishijima found himself on the verge of being retired again; Father went to Sendai to plead for Hishijima and got into heated discussion with the division commander. Consequently, whenever Hishijima as brigade commander sent in his recommendations for promotion, the division commander always struck out Father's name. Finally Hishijima was retired and the division commander sent his own chief of staff to replace Hishijima. As a result, Father was transferred off to Fukushima.

Much later I heard my father tell someone that Hishijima was reactivated again during the Russo-Japanese War. Then, on several occasions, Hishijima sent sums of 10,000 or 20,000 yen home from the battlefront to his creditors.[10] By the time he returned he had not only repaid all his debts but had also built up a sizable fortune.

My father's house in Fukushima was right next to the regimental headquarters. It was the smallest and shabbiest house our family had ever lived in. No maids were provided and so my younger sister had been forced to quit school to look after the house and my numerous brothers and sisters.

The thing that shocked me the most, however, was the tremendous change that had taken place in my father. He was still only forty-two or forty-three but had suddenly aged. Now he seemed like an old man long past fifty. And whereas he had always left the management of the household entirely in Mother's hands and we had never so much as heard him

10. This equaled $5,000 to $10,000 U.S. in this period.

say a word about money matters, now he had joined the money-worshippers.

He had always lived simply, never carrying even pocket money with him—indeed, he had never before known how money was used. Perhaps this is why his stinginess had never shown itself earlier. Perhaps it suddenly materialized after Mother died and he tried to keep track of the details of the family finances.

In any case, he now said that he couldn't possibly manage on his monthly salary combined with the annuity he received from being decorated. He was mystified, he said, as to how Mother had ever managed such a fine life all those years, usually even having something left over every month. This worry about money and raising so many children without a mother was what had aged Father so quickly. Now he suddenly began to appreciate money.

If what Father's elder brother told me later was true, Father got to the point of considering abandoning his military career and finding other employment, even in the business world. Now when Father read the daily newspaper he perused the stock market reports first. He also urged me to read them and even gave me lessons about how to understand them. I began to wonder when he could have learned about such things. Actually he had a tutor who was responsible for this new enthusiasm about business and newspaper columns on the stock market. One day I went with him to visit whoever was the colonel or lieutenant colonel serving as regimental commander. The regimental commander gave the exact same lesson that Father had given me.

I felt pity for my father when I saw how old and tired he had become. But I could not sympathize with his change in thinking; rather I felt contempt. When I heard that his tutor was the regimental commander, I was filled with indignation and scorn at the thought that the whole army had sunk so low.

Thus my homecoming after a long absence turned out not to be a very happy one. After about a month I went back to Tokyo.

I no sooner entered the Foreign Language College than I met disappointment. I had taken two and a half years of French in military school and had been studying for many more months in night classes at the

French Language School. Even though I didn't understand everything, I had been reading books in French. Now I discovered that I was supposed to begin all over again, starting with the alphabet.

Thanks to a Frenchman named Jacques Rey teaching there, after a half-month of this I was allowed to advance to the second-year course as a special student with the promise of graduating as a regular student. But the second-year course didn't amount to much more than the first. It was when I went to this second-year course that I became aware how absurd the teachers were. I was shocked. Teachers who said that they had spent ten or fifteen years in France could not do what a second-year student could do. They had covered their books with penciled notes and gave their lectures by picking out sections to read to us. They were utterly unable to answer if a pupil asked something that they could not find in their books. The only two teachers who knew anything were lazy and rarely came to class; if they did come, they merely lectured us on etiquette. There were numerous instructors but I had almost no contact with any of them.

Only one, Jacques Rey, was really enthusiastic. During his daily two hours he lectured on anything and everything. I decided that just listening to his lectures would be enough and stayed away from the classes with the other teachers as much as possible.

War clouds were steadily gathering between Russia and Japan about this period. A craze of patriotism swept the nation. Even the *Yorozu Chōhō News,* which alone had previously maintained an attitude of calm, suddenly changed its tone. Kōtoku, Sakai, and Uchimura Kanzō together published a bitter farewell message and left the paper.[11] Then Kōtoku and Sakai founded the weekly paper *Commoners News* and began to champion the causes of socialism and pacifism.

Until then my contact with these men had been through their newspaper articles and the eloquent speeches that they made at the oc-

11. Sakai is identified in chapter 1 note 2, Kōtoku in chapter 5 note 9. Uchimura (1861–1930) was a very prominent Christian social reformer who first gained fame for his resignation from teaching at the elite First Higher School in a dispute over how to show proper respect toward the emperor. He became a successful author and senior editor of the *Yorozu Chōhō News.*

casional meetings in the main hall of the Hongō church. I had never met them personally. Now, however, I decided I wanted to join the ranks of the army they were raising. Kōtoku's book *The Essence of Socialism* had set my brain on fire.[12]

One cold snowy night I went to Sukiyabashi to visit the Commoners Society for the first time. It was the night for the regular meeting of the Socialist Study Group that was held there every week.

As I entered the vestibule, straight off to the left was a six- or eight-mat room with three or four men; they all seemed to be at ease there. Two of them, a young man and an older man, were arguing intently about something. I said nothing but sat down with my back against the wall a little removed from the rest. The discussion seemed to be about the issue of religion. The older man was sitting cross-legged, resting an elbow on one knee and rubbing his head as he ridiculed his younger adversary and gave vent to what sounded like atheistic remarks. The younger man sat very straight, his hands placed on his knees, his shoulders hunched forward angrily, and his face vivid red as he literally spewed forth a ludicrous orthodoxy. Another older man, who I knew immediately must be Sakai, occasionally interrupted to argue with the younger man, but his remarks were not nearly so pointed as those of the first man.

I was surprised by the eloquence that gushed from the lips of the younger man. But I was even more surprised by the extreme orthodoxy of his argument. I was a Christian just as he was. But I didn't really believe in miracles whereas he, by contrast, believed in the Bible word for word. I believed that God was something within ourselves but he believed that God was above all things, governing them. I wondered how such a person had ever come to socialism. Thus I was more in sympathy with the derision expressed by the man who seemed to be an atheist. This was Katsumi Kesson. The younger man was Yamaguchi Koken.[13]

12. This work, *Shakaishugi shinzui*, was published in 1903.
13. Katsumi (1860–1925) was another journalist on the newspaper *Yorozu Chōhō*. Ōsugi later sided with radicals like Kōtoku and Sakai. Yamaguchi Gizō (1883–1920), also a journalist, remained an active Socialist until his death; see chapter 1 note 1.

Before long some twenty others had assembled and the man I thought must be Sakai spoke to us.

"Since it is snowing and there are many new faces here tonight, let us dispense with the lecture and talk freely among ourselves about such things as how our circumstances led each of us to enter socialism."

We each rose in turn and said something. One man stated, "I am the son of a capitalist. During the Sino-Japanese War there was much talk about Ōkura's canned goods having stones in them. Those were cans from our place. But we didn't do it; apparently it was done according to Ōkura's scheme."

Sakai then said, "In that case they *were* really Ōkura's canned goods, weren't they? Rather than saying it was done at your place, it would make a better story if you said Ōkura's did it. So let's make it Ōkura's, shall we!"

Everyone broke into laughter and agreed: "True! True! It was Ōkura's!"

The capitalist's son was named Henmi something and he is now the head of the Kenshi Milk Company.

My turn came almost last: "I was raised in a military family and I've been taught in a military school, and I am at the point that I feel I've floated in the lies and absurdity of military life. Therefore I want to devote my life [*to the socialist movement*]."[14]

After everyone had spoken, Sakai arose and gave a stirring address. "Here we have the son of the military; there the son of capitalists; here, the son of one; there, of another. Now our ideas are spreading to all corners of the globe. Thus our movement is becoming the great movement of the world. The day when our ideal society will be here is not far off."

As I heard those words I felt their truth. That night as I returned to my lodgings I experienced a wonderful feeling.

I don't know whether Kōtoku was present that night or not. Every week after that, without fail, I attended the meetings of the study group. I also went there on other days, especially after I moved in with Tosaka

14. The words in brackets were censored in the 1930 Kaizō edition.

and Tanaka in Tsukishima. I would stop in almost daily on my way home from school and spent the rest of the day helping with activities such as addressing mailing wrappers.

VI.

In the Commoners Society were Kōtoku, Sakai, Nishikawa Kōjirō, and Ishikawa Sanshirō.[15] Of the four, only Ishikawa did not despise religion. But there were outsiders who supported the society who were enthusiastic Christians like Ishikawa: that is, Abe Isoo and Kinoshita Yōkō.[16] Moreover, the majority of the youths who came were Christians. After all, Christian ideas were the most progressive in the intellectual world of the day. Or, at least, Christianity contained the most numerous elements in rebellion against the ideas of loyalty and patriotism then dominant.

Kōtoku and Sakai sneered at and made scathing attacks on religion. They often brought up religious issues at the study group meetings. Nonetheless both Kōtoku and Sakai accepted the resolution of the German Social Democratic party, which held that religion was an individual's private concern, and they did not actually interfere with their comrades' religion.

Ishikawa was my senior at the Hongō church. About that time, however, he seemed to lose all interest in church and stopped going entirely. After I began going to the Commoners Society, under its influence I too became increasingly skeptical—first about religious people and then about religion itself. The war between Russia and Japan cleanly severed my ties with religion.

I had believed, as Ebina Danjō taught, that religion had a *cosmopolitanism* that transcended national boundaries and a *libertarianism*

15. Nishikawa Mitsujirō (1876–1940) and Ishikawa Sanshirō (Kyokuzan, 1876–1956) were both important left-wing militants.

16. Abe (1865–1959) and Kinoshita Naoe (1869–1937) were prominent Christian socialists who opposed the war and who influenced Ōsugi (see chapter 5 part 3). Abe was a professor at Waseda University, where he also became known as the father of Japanese baseball. Kinoshita, a graduate of Waseda, gained a reputation as a journalist for his 1899–1900 reports on the Ashio Copper pollution case and as a novelist with his 1904 *Hi no Hashira* (Pillar of fire).

that recognized no temporal authority.[17] Tolstoy's views on religion, which had come into vogue in intellectual circles at the time, strengthened my beliefs on this. Moreover, after reading about the origins of Christianity in Ebina Danjō's *Life of Christ* and in *The Life of Buddha* written by a doctor of Buddhism, I had thought it was as Tolstoy had said: primitive religion—in other words, real religion—was a variety of communist movement attempting to escape the insecurity in society that stems from the gulf between the rich and the poor.

But the attitude that religious individuals took toward the war—especially the attitude of Ebina in whom I believed—thoroughly betrayed my faith. The fact that Ebina's Christianity was one of nationalism and the Japanese spirit was now clearly exposed to my sight. He held prayer meetings for victory. He sang hymns that seemed like military songs. He gave sermons on loyalty and patriotism. And he quoted Christ completely out of context, as in "I came not to bring peace."[18]

I grew thoroughly disgusted. After several arguments with Ebina and with Katō Yokushi, who had translated a great many of Tolstoy's works, I turned my back on churches once and for all. Simultaneously I came to doubt the principle of nonresistance, the "turn the other cheek" that is an essential quality of religion and that I had begun unconsciously to embrace. Thus I could now embrace pure socialism and the class struggle.

When the war broke out, my father was immediately made a battalion commander in one of the mixed brigades of a reserve division and was dispatched to the Liaotung Peninsula. I went to meet him when his brigade passed through Ueno Station and stayed overnight with him at his inn.

When I saw Father on horseback directing his troops, the first time that he had cut such a heroic figure, the sight almost moved even me to tears. But there was also something ridiculous to me about it when I thought to myself, What is the purpose [*of going courageously to*

17. The words in italics are foreign in the original.
18. See Matt. 10:34, "Think not that I am come to send peace on earth; I came not to send peace, but a sword."

war]?[19] Rather than feel sorry for Father, I felt that the scene was ludicrous.

Once we entered the inn my father and the old-timers among the officers in his command went about in high spirits cheerfully telling everyone they met, "This is our last campaign."

Father had very little to say to me that night except "Study hard." It seemed to be enough for him to have me sitting by his side and to see my face.

19. The words in brackets were censored in the 1930 Kaizō edition.

LIFE IN PRISON
1906-1910

I. ICHIGAYA

In Tokyo Jail, where they keep the accused awaiting trial, was an old guard nicknamed Repeaters.[1] Whenever we were summoned to court as defendants, we were lined up along a wide dimly lit corridor before being put together with a dozen or so others into a horse-drawn van (now I suppose the job is done by automobile). In the corridor our hands were shackled in manacles chained to our waists, and roll was called out by the head of the escort section. Then the old guard referred to as Repeaters took over as one of the two escorts for each group. I do not know how long he had been assigned to escort duty or when he had received his nickname. But surely he had been eating prison food for at least thirty years and must have been somewhere close to sixty.

When we defendants were assembled in the corridor this guard took the roster from the jailer in charge. Although tall and heavy, he took short quick steps as he moved about checking not only the faces of each

---

1. Although often treated as chapter 7 of the *Autobiography*, these prison reminiscences were published separately as *Prison Memoirs* (*Gokuchūki* and *Gokuchūki zoku*) in early 1919, almost three years before the first six chapters appeared. For more on Ōsugi's life in prison from other sources, see Stanley, *Ōsugi Sakae*, chap. 4.

Tokyo Jail was in the Ichigaya district.

of those in his own group but those in the other group as well. This so-called roster actually consisted of a card for each defendant that recorded such things as family of origin, social status, criminal offenses, and physical description.

The guard, after looking over many of the others, stopped abruptly in front of the man next to me. "I've seen you before, haven't I?" he said. He stared at the prisoner for some time, his small eyes seemingly good-natured and his dark, homely face guileless. Finally he said, "Yes; it was when you were in Osaka." The guard spoke familiarly but in a tone of voice that seemed to say the prisoner was presuming on his good nature.

The prisoner, who had remained silent with a surprised look on his face, now rubbed his hands together as if the manacles cramped them and answered: "No, sir. Please don't joke. This is the first time I have ever been in such a place."

The guard showed no sign of anger as he told him, "Don't lie." Suddenly the guard smiled, his eyes shining a bit more, and he nodded and spoke half to himself. "That's it. It was surely Osaka. And after that you were brought in once in Kofu City."

"No sir! You're mistaken. This is my first time ever." The prisoner rubbed his hands together even harder, bowing deeply.

"Come on! It won't do to keep pretending." The old guard went on, paying no attention to the other man's protests. "There was also another time when you were in Sugamo Prison. Then there was one other time—where was that?"

This hit the mark. The prisoner stopped rubbing his hands together and said only, "Yes."

"Where was it?"

"It was at Chiba, sir."

Everyone else thought he was a first offender—the arresting officer as well as those down at police headquarters and the authorities at the procurator's office. But it turned out that he actually had four prior arrests. I heard the whole amazing exchange from the start. Afterward he whispered to me, "I just couldn't stand up to that one."

This last March when I returned briefly to Tokyo Jail it was just as it had been that March twelve years earlier when I first saw it.[2] Repeaters carried on as before—his face a bit darker, a bit more homely, but smiling as good-naturedly as ever. "Well, here you are again. It's been a long while since I've seen you. What's it for this time?" Now I look back on that old guard with nostalgia but then, as a repeat offender, I felt fear.

Actually I don't remember it all that well. During the previous three or four months I had been called down to the procurator's office several times to be interrogated about matters involving rice riots and newspaper articles. I too was unable to give any satisfactory reply about my own previous arrests. When the procurator read me the record I simply answered, "You've investigated and I assume you have all the details correctly recorded." That ended it, as he cordially replied, "Well, that's probably so." But later when I thought it over, I realized that there were errors in the procurator's investigation—for some reason they had me down for one arrest too few.

It would not be difficult to check on these court cases by simply looking in the newspapers and magazines of the day, but it would be a nuisance so I shall simply put down the crimes and sentences as I recall them now. I don't recall the exact days or months and years when I went in or got out. And I have forgotten all the prison numbers I wore except the first one: that was 979. This is not true of me alone. Ask Sakai (Toshihiko) or Yamakawa (Hitoshi) or Yamaguchi (Koken) or any of the other of my colleagues who have been arrested three or four times.[3] None of them can give you the details either. Thus the following list of violations of the original Press Ordinances (which differed from the present Press Laws) is merely from my own memory.

1. Violation of the Press Ordinances
    (Endangering the Public Order)—3 months

2. In March 1918 Ōsugi was arrested for interfering with a police officer in the Yoshiwara district; he describes the incident below. He was again arrested in March 1919 for a violation of the Press Laws.

3. On Sakai and Yamaguchi see chapter 1 notes 1, 2; on Yamakawa (1880–1958), another young member of the Socialist movement, see chapter 5 note 7.

2. Violation of the Press Ordinances
   (Attacking the Constitution)—5 months

3. Violation of the Peace Preservation Act
   (Rooftop Speech Incident)—1½ months

4. Seditious Rioting
   (Streetcar Fare Incident)—2 years

5. Obstructing Officials and Violation of the Peace Preservation
   Law
   (Red Flags Incident)—2½ years[4]

According to this, there were five offenses and nearly six years in sentences. In reality I served a little over three years. That is only one-tenth the thirty years served by Breshkovskaya, the "grandmother of revolution" who visited Japan recently.[5] Sakai, Yamakawa, Yamaguchi, and I all had roughly the same number of convictions but Yamaguchi and Yamakawa served about a year or two longer. I was by far the junior of all my comrades.

My first stretch came in my twenty-second spring as a result of the Seditious Rioting Incident. The Japanese Socialist party was in existence (today there is no such party) and held a citizens' rally to oppose the increase in streetcar fares (up from three to five sen each way). I was arrested at the end of March, held for trial, and then released on bail in June. The other four incidents all took place during the two-year period

4. Between 1868 and World War I the Meiji government attempted a variety of approaches to censoring the press. Mitchell sums up the relevant laws in *Censorship in Imperial Japan*, whose translations of these terms I generally follow. Ōsugi's memory was indeed not always accurate; for one example see Stanley, *Ōsugi Sakae*, 186 n.32. *First violation:* published the translation of a French article that advocated resisting the military draft in November 1906 issue of the left-wing magazine *Hikari* (The Light). *Second violation:* published translations from the writings of Pyotr Kropotkin, the Russian anarchist, in March 1907 issues of the left-wing newspaper *Heimin Shinbun*. *Third violation:* arrested on 17 January 1908; after the police broke up a Socialist meeting, Ōsugi joined Sakai Toshihiko and Yamakawa Hitoshi on the roof of the building, where they defied police orders to stop making public speeches. *Fourth violation:* arrested on 15 March 1906; see chapter 6 note 3. *Fifth violation:* see chapter 1 note 1.

5. Catherine Breshkovsky (E. R. Breshkovskaya, 1844–1934), imprisoned and exiled to Siberia under the czar, was released in 1917 by the Kerensky regime. As Ōsugi did, she later rejected the Bolshevik program.

when I was still on bail for that Seditious Rioting Incident. The nine and a half months I did for the first three incidents were served while my other cases were pending.

In the periods between being repeatedly jailed and released I was out for two or, at the longest, six months. Finally, I was arrested in the summer of my twenty-fourth year for waving those red flags with "[anarchism and communism]" at the Kinkikan Hall,[6] and this was combined with the time owed for the streetcar incident. Thanks to the old penal code in force at that time, these three were combined into concurrent offenses and given precedence in the judgment over the two cases of Press Ordinance violations. Thus the two years for the Streetcar Fare Incident and the month and a half I had already served for the Rooftop Speech Incident were subsumed into the two-and-a-half-year sentence for the Red Flags Incident. In other words, these others added up to zero!

I heard that down at the procurators' office they were jumping up and down in frustration. Probably they were. Though I was still on bail when picked up three other times, they completely forgot. Thanks to that, I had walked off with a prize. It was not something you can get away with anymore. Under the present new penal code, which went into effect in October of that year, no matter how many crimes are involved, each must now be dealt with entirely separately.

At the end of my twenty-seventh year, just a month before Kōtoku and the other rebels were sentenced to death, I once again saw the outside.[7] Ever since, for all of seven years, I have been on my best behavior. Altogether, off and on, my life in prison spanned six years from the spring of my twenty-second year to the end of my twenty-seventh. Hence my notorious reputation as a dangerous character—which I am accorded even now that I have reached the mature age of thirty-four—

6. The words in brackets were censored in the 1930 Kaizō edition; the reference is to the 1908 Red Flags Incident, sometimes called the Kinkikan Incident because it began at this hall in Tokyo's Kanda district.

7. In November 1910 Kōtoku and others among Ōsugi's circle were convicted for conspiring to assassinate the emperor (see Fred G. Notehelfer, *Kōtoku Shūsui*, chaps. 7, 8). Had he not been in jail when the alleged conspiracy took place, Ōsugi might well have been indicted with them.

really stems from the impetuous follies of a youthful spirit committed between the spring of my twenty-second and the end of my twenty-fourth year.

There was one other time, however, when I unexpectedly visited Tokyo Jail—a time that had nothing to do with impetuous folly or youthful spirit. In fact it ended with even the authorities making their apologies. This happened last year and I want to provide the details.

On the evening of the first of March there was a small gathering of comrades at the Ueno home of a colleague. It was too late to catch a Kameido streetcar home, so Hisaita and I decided to stay with Wada at his cheap inn at Furusu in the Namidabashi district.[8] Thus we were tramping along on foot between Minowa and Nihonzutsumi. Now Wada and Hisaita are both doing their first stretches in Tokyo Jail for violating the Press Ordinances. The "Portrait of Mr. H" that was exhibited this year by Hayashi Shizue at the Nikakai was a portrait of this same Hisaita. As we passed before the main gate of the Yoshiwara district,[9] we came on a crowd of people milling about. One man, who seemed to be a laborer, had drunk too much and they said he had accidentally broken the glass window of a bar. Someone was demanding that the neighborhood patrol or the police seize the man and jail him until he paid for the damage. The man, who looked wretched, staggered about trying desperately to apologize.

Seeing this, I intervened. I took the man a few steps to the side, listened to his explanations, and then addressed those gathered there.

"This man hasn't a penny on him now. I'll pay the damages. That should be the end of it. It's no good to go calling the police every time something happens. As far as possible we shouldn't call the authorities. Most things can be settled this way by the people who are on the spot."

The people from the bar agreed to that. The neighborhood patrol also agreed. The onlookers too agreed. The only person who could not

8. In the spring of 1918 Wada Kyūtarō (1893–1928) and Hisaita Unosuke (1877–1922) joined Ōsugi in publishing a labor newspaper called *Rōdō Shinbun*.

9. Once the center for theaters, geisha, and other urbane culture, the Yoshiwara district by this time had become most noted for its houses of prostitution.

agree was the policeman. He had been staring at me from the beginning
with a sullen expression and now challenged me.

"The gentleman is talking socialism, aren't you?"

"I am. So what?" I challenged him back.

"It's socialism, so you're under arrest. Come with me."

"This is humorous! I'll go wherever you want." I shoved the policeman's hand away and rushed into the Nihonzutsumi police station,
which was just across from us. There, an assistant inspector ordered the
policeman to take me to the detention hall along with the other two who
had followed us. This incident was reported in one newspaper at the
time as "ŌSUGI AND OTHERS ARRESTED," turning the simple facts into
a string of fabrications and writing that, while intoxicated and cruising
the Yoshiwara, we interfered with a policeman taking custody of a
drunkard and then tried to flee with the drunkard.

The next morning an inspector came and apologized profusely for
the misunderstanding, sending in a splendid breakfast for us and saying,
"Please go home without further fuss." But as we were about to leave,
a superintendent showed up and for some reason we were taken back
again to the detention hall. Thus, like guests at cheap inns, we spent two
nights in the station house, another night at police headquarters, and
five more nights in Tokyo Jail on the charge of interfering with an officer
doing his duty. After all this they sent us home with the polite farewell,
"We are quite sorry. Please go on your way."

By nature I almost never take a drink and have never in my entire life
paid for a prostitute. My disposition is so timid that in reality I always
lose even when wrestling with a lady.[10]

Then this last summer, just a week after I returned from observing
the rice riots in Osaka,[11] they said, "Let's go down to the station." I was
taken straight to Idabashi police station and then spent ten days at headquarters officially "in custody." Again, it was not that I had done anything wrong while in Osaka or that any suspicion existed about any-

10. Ōsugi may refer here to the 1916 scandal when he was seriously wounded by his
lover, Kamichika Ichiko.

11. Beginning in August 1918 Osaka and other areas of Japan were rocked by
large-scale and sometimes violent consumer protests.

thing I had done since returning to Tokyo. It was just time for the authorities, in their kindness, to do something to let the police and army rattle their sabers.

Every mealtime, three times a day, I was taken to a beautiful sitting room and the station chief would come to take my order. Each day he would bring along a woman to keep me company and would say with a straight face, "I regret that it has to be such a place but there is nothing at all to be concerned about. What do you say, madam? Wouldn't you like to stay the night too?"

I ended up almost trusting him myself. The newspapers went on about how I had been arrested while making a speech in the streets of Osaka. The whole story, root and branch, was just mischief on the part of journalists.

On other occasions, more than I can count, I was detained in this way out of the kindness of the authorities. It was not a matter of whether I had done something wrong or something right. In any case, whatever I was doing and whatever the place, if I was doing it then there was going to be a misunderstanding. That is the one point I would like to state at the outset in my defense.

"All right, inside."

The padlock was opened and the door swung back with a horrendous noise. I followed the guard's orders and stepped in carrying the bedding and clothes box they had issued me.

"Put the box on the shelf. Now the pillow goes here, and spread out the quilts here. Good. I'll tell you about the rest tomorrow. Get to sleep now." Then with a dreadful rattling and clanging that echoed not only through the room but throughout the building, he closed the door behind him.

This is it, my home, I thought, and stayed standing for a first look around. It was a snug room, just three mats in size. On the floor were two unbound tatami mats and planks along the wall under the window opposite the entrance. In the corner to the right of the window stood a washstand with a spigot and an iron washbowl. Below it hung a broom, a dustpan, and a scrub rag. There was also something that looked like a scrub bucket. In the floor of the left-hand corner was a plank with a hole just big enough for a finger. Wondering what it was for, I pulled the plank up and looked in. The bottom, a foot or so below, was concrete, and set into the very middle was a narrow wooden cover about a foot long with a small handle on it. When I lifted the cover the stench surged up. A latrine. I quickly stepped down and took a piss. It sounded like it hit an empty bucket. Putting the cover back on, I washed my hands at the spigot. The window, about three feet high and four feet wide, was placed so far up in the wall that you could see out only by straining up. Through the glass pane the night was pitch-black without a single star. At two-foot intervals along all four sides of the room were three-inch-wide boards set into the walls. From the high ceiling in the middle of the room hung, shining brightly, a five-candlepower bulb.

This is first class. *Comfortable and convenient—the simple life!* I said to myself.[12] I hung the towel from a bar fastened to the shelf on the wall to the left and, adjusting the string belt on the blue kimono they had given me to change into, I started to crawl into bed. I wonder where the others are? I thought about the ten comrades who had been hauled in with me from the citizens' rally several days before. So I went to peer out at the corridor through the peephole set in the upper part of the door. This was the corridor I had scrutinized when looking for my companions as I was brought to my cell. About a dozen feet across the way, stretching on either side as far as I could see, were doors like giant faces: a peephole above for an eye, a six-inch-square food slot below for a mouth, and, dangling from the door bolt in the middle like a nose, one of the huge brightly polished padlocks that made such fearful noises. The lights within the cells beyond shone through the eyes into the dim corridor and caused the bridge of each nose to glisten. The narrow peepholes that pierced the three-inch-thick doors were made for peering into a cell and were no good for looking out from it. So I crouched down and used my fingernails to open the food slot. Now I could see from one end

12. The words in italics are in English in the original.

of the building to the other; there were even more giant faces than I had been able to see before. But nowhere among the eyes of those twenty-some odd faces could I see what I hoped for—a real human eye looking out. It was thus a bit eerie to have only those giant faces staring back at me.

They're probably all asleep. I'll get some sleep too. Everything can wait till morning. I used my fingernails to close the slot and immediately crawled into bed. In only underclothes with the single cotton quilt, I shivered in the cold.

Suddenly I shot straight up—there was a knocking from the wall on the right-hand side of my cell. It came again—knock, knock, knock— like someone rapping on the wallboard with his fist. I had read in books that Russian comrades in prison carried on conversations by knocking this way. This must be one of the comrades from whom I had been separated now talking to me from the next cell.

"You're Ōsugi, right?"

I tried to imitate his low tone and answered, "Yes, I am. Who are you?" The voice, which sounded like that of a child, was not one I recognized—a man I did not know. Yet he knew my name though I had just been brought in. Still, this did not strike me as surprising.

"It doesn't matter who I am. I am just speaking for my neighbor next door. They've all been waiting for you for days. When we heard just now about a new arrival he guessed it was you and asked me to check."

"What's the name of your next-door neighbor?"

"It's a fellow named X[13] who's in for the incendiary case. He and Yamaguchi, the comrade across the corridor, go together every day when they are taken for baths or exercise. So Yamaguchi asked him to ask about you."

"Can I talk with Yamaguchi?"

"Sure. Please wait a bit. The guard's on his break so I'll try to talk with my neighbor."

13. Either Ōsugi or the censor deleted this name. If the text refers to the Hibiya incendiary riots of September 1905, there is some irony here. Those riots were in protest against the Portsmouth peace treaty with Russia, a war that Ōsugi and his comrades opposed.

After a while I was told to open the food slot and look out. I did right away and across the corridor I could see half of Yamaguchi's spectacled face looking back from a food slot three doors away.

"Over here. Well, you got here! What about Sakai? Is he all right?"

"He's all right. Nothing happened to him."

"That's great. Any of the others brought in with you?"

"No, just me," I answered. "Where is everybody else? What about Nishikawa (Kōjirō)?"[14]

"Sh, sh."

Yamaguchi poked his face further out to warn me and then pulled back and disappeared from the slot. From a distance I could hear footsteps. I quickly got back into bed. I listened to the footsteps come closer until they seemed very near my head, then gradually fade into the distance again.

Knock, knock, knock on the wall came again from next door. My neighbor then served as a conduit for conversation with the man on the other side of him. This way I learned that Nishikawa and two or three others were on the second floor and one other comrade was here on the same side of the corridor as we were.

I found it all fascinating. Since my arrest the evening before I had been filled with curiosity about going to prison for the first time. All along the way, as I was taken from the police station to the detention hall, from jail to the procurator's office, from that office to this prison, I had looked forward to finding out what kind of place it would be and what would happen to me in it.

Here I could rest fully content. My earlier determination to remain calm and composed was bolstered by having my comrades in such close proximity. Even wrapped only in a single quilt I could ignore the cold and the cramped quarters. After tossing about once or twice with these thoughts in my head I fell sound asleep.

It was raining the next day and we could not go outside to exercise. So men were let out three or four at a time to walk up and down the

14. Nishikawa Mitsujirō (Kōjirō, 1876–1940) was a left-wing militant and belonged to the Commoners Society.

corridor. Once again I opened up the slot and watched the others as they walked along the corridor. I exchanged nods with Yamaguchi and the man with whom I had communicated through my neighbor the night before. When I was let out with my neighbor, he immediately told me that the other man walking with us was Noguchi Osaburō, the man who had committed the famous Noguchi murders.[15] Osaburō also asked about me, and when we came face to face he nodded to me.

I formed a bond with Osaburō. Over the next two and a half years while he was awaiting execution, we became close although we never spoke a single word. During that period I was brought in and let out two or three different times, and he too was always put in Tokyo Jail to stay at least one night whenever they brought him over from the prison in Sugamo to appear in court. Osaburō gave me support at a time when we were equally convicts who had lost our freedom. I would often receive something through the food slot from him—a sheet of writing paper or a piece of bread—either from Osaburō directly or indirectly through one of the prisoners who worked for the guards as a trusty. And when I was on the outside I would send him in a book on something or other.

Even among the other prisoners Osaburō had a terrible reputation. He was always intent on currying favor with any officials from the warden on down. Some said that was why he became a favorite of theirs and why his execution kept being put off. Outside the interrogation room was a place you were put to wait your turn—it was only six feet square and we called it the bird cage. On one of the wooden slats inside someone had scratched with his fingernail the righteous words, BEHEAD THE MONSTER OSABURŌ NOW.

Perhaps by becoming close to someone like me he was also trying to get the attention of society. In prison I actually received one or two letters that suggested this explanation. It is also what the comrades who were in with me were always saying.

In any case, Osaburō was a very tender-hearted man. Whenever someone mentioned either the boy or the daughter of his brother-in-

15. In May 1905 Noguchi Osaburō was arrested for the murder of a pharmacist and was also charged in the death of his brother-in-law, Noguchi Neisai, killed that same month. He was subsequently blamed for the 1902 murder of an eleven-year-old boy, parts of whose flesh had been eaten; this case had great notoriety.

law, he always wept. It was said that he kept near him at all times a photograph of the child, which he once showed to me. It was also said that he himself had done a drawing of the girl and the boy and he once displayed a colored picture of the sort you see in magazines. Certainly it looked like something traced from a magazine. But I wonder how he got hold of the pigments to do it. He would have had to go to a lot of pains to extract and collect them. What was his purpose in going to all that trouble? Besides, these were not pictures of the girl or the boy in the case; they had different faces that bore no resemblance to them.

I was very happy when it was decided that there was insufficient evidence to convict him of the murder of his brother-in-law. There was also talk that, in the murder of the pharmacist, an accomplice masterminded the whole thing and actually did the killing but that the accomplice had the assistance of a lawyer and was even getting his daily meals sent in from the outside. I also heard that on one occasion in the courtroom Osaburō became furious at the man and struck out at him.

Later on, when I was in awaiting trial on the Red Flags Incident, I was walking about in the exercise yard when Osaburō's face appeared at a second-story window. He held up a piece of some kind of paper on which was written in large letters, "Praying for health." I silently acknowledged it by nodding my head. Osaburō gave two or three bows and remained gazing in my direction for some time, beaming his usual lonely but amiable smile.

That next day, or the day after that, word spread through the prison that Osaburō was finally done for.

While in I also met Buck-Toothed Turtle.[16] Actually the man's teeth did not protrude that much. He looked rather seedy, always grinning as he shuffled along with his back hunched over. Everyone called out, "Hey, Buck-Toothed Turtle" or some such, but he just kept on grinning. After he was sentenced one of the guards asked: "Hey, Buck-Toothed Turtle! How many years you get?"

16. This nickname, *Debakame,* is the colloquial term for sexual assailant and involves a pun on the name Kintarō. The press attached it to Ikeda Kintarō in another notorious murder case; Ikeda was one of two men arrested in March 1908 for fatally assaulting a woman as she walked home from the public bath.

"Life!" he answered, laughing.

There were three men with whom I exercised and bathed and who became my close prison friends. One was a large fat man in his forties who had been convicted of robbery and murder but whose death sentence had been commuted to life imprisonment in Hokkaido. He escaped, was arrested for a second robbery-murder, and was again sentenced to death. A second friend, also in his forties, was a delicate-looking man who had the air of a nobleman. He had been brought up from Kyoto to appeal his forgery case to either the appellate court or the Supreme Court. The third was a dignified old man in his sixties with grey hair who was a swindler. He had been brought in after me and became one of our group.

The murderer often talked about the time he had escaped in Hokkaido. He had hidden in the hills for about a month and told us he had eaten the buds and roots of trees or whatever else he could find. "There's nothing you can't eat, friend!" he would declare and roll his tiny eyes as he rubbed the whiskers that, for lack of a razor, had been growing ever since he arrived. He was always demanding his own way, saying "After all, I don't know when I may be hanged." And if he could not have something he would make a commotion as if any moment he would run amok. He stayed in the bath longer than anyone else and he exercised longer than anyone else. Thanks to him, our group got away with a great deal. Facing him, even the most demonic guard quickly turned into an angel. If a guard spoke roughly to a convict or an accused, this fellow would stand up like one of Buddha's guardian kings and start to shout and carry on until another guard arrived to placate him. And yet if he was handled with a little care, he became as gentle as a kitten and sweet as a child.

On one occasion, I heard that he was looking out his window and saw a female guard pass by, escorting some women accused or detainees. The guard, who was scolding and prodding them along from behind, lifted her hat while glancing in the direction of the men's window. This fellow saw her and began to shout, "Itō, you witch! You old witch! You old witch!" He shouted himself hoarse for the rest of the day. Even today, when I have forgotten the names of all the other guards, I still hear him in my head calling her name: Itō. She was a tall woman and rather old. On that occasion I too saw the women, standing on my scrub bucket in order to gaze at them.

When among us friends this murderer was extremely pleasant, but on one occasion he berated the forger. The forger spent a long time in Manchuria and ran a whorehouse there. From time to time he would take as his spouse one of the local geisha whom he had met somewhere. And, we heard, he would then even have his own woman sell herself. One day in the middle of the exercise yard, the murderer got very angry and began to bawl him out.

"You're a bastard! Making your own wife sell herself! What an ass! I've stolen; I've set fires; I've even killed. But I've never done anything so bad as making my own woman sell herself! Didn't you think that was even a little wrong? Didn't it disgust you?"

The old swindler and I stepped in to mediate and after a while we calmed him down. While being shouted at, the forger remained silent. Then, trembling a bit and his face pale, he responded with candor.

"No. As a matter of fact, I didn't feel I was doing anything wrong. And I still don't think it was wrong. It was the natural thing to do and I would do it again today. My woman was always the biggest moneymaker."

At this the dignified old swindler, a lecher who we heard always chose sixteen or seventeen year olds as his mistresses, opened his mouth and began to laugh delightedly. The murderer made an indignant expression as if he was disgusted at us all, but then he finally started to laugh along with the old swindler.

The old swindler and the forger got along very well. Walking together, they would tell stories about the crimes they had committed and would brag about the amounts of money they had made in the take. The forger claimed he had once counterfeited Russian banknotes and realized a great return. The old swindler had done things like expunging the cancellations on revenue stamps and reselling them. The swindler suggested, "Next time we're out of here, let's try counterfeiting using photographs the way you did," and he asked the forger to explain in detail how to use photography.

I often shared the eggs and bread I got from outside with the murderer and enjoyed listening to the tall tales he told so guilelessly. Nothing happened to him for three or four years after his sentencing. I think that was because he had not exhausted his appeals. Afterward, I understand, his sentence was reduced to life in prison and he was sent back to Hokkaido.

II. SUGAMO

In the ordinary world, Destination Sugamo simply refers to a streetcar and doesn't have much to do with most people's lives. For us, however, it means Destination Prison.[17] When I say *us* I mean those of us who are treated by the ordinary world as if quite crazy. Maybe however you look at it, it comes to the same thing.

I was sent to Sugamo a total of three times—well, actually two times. While I was under my first sentence for violation of the Press Ordinances I was sentenced again for the same offense.[18] I began serving my second sentence immediately on finishing the first. The other time was for violating the Peace Preservation Law.

I think it was probably at Kajibashi that the old lockup stood. When they tore it down, they used the stones and bricks to build the new prison here. And it is said that they used the original timbers to reconstruct one of the old buildings off to one corner. This building was also the infirmary where they put the blind, the crippled, the old men who couldn't get around very well, the disabled, and semi-invalids. Twice I was transferred to a large cell inside that building.

The first time I was brought from Tokyo Jail and put into one of those dark cold cells, it disheartened me. It was midday in the spring and the sun shone with the warmth of early summer. Nevertheless, as I entered that room I suddenly felt throughout my body the chill in the air. One look at the four walls of whitewashed brick and the large iron-plated door on the entrance made me shudder. When I reached out to

17. This prison was in the Sugamo district of Tokyo.
18. For publications in November 1906 and March 1907 Ōsugi was charged with violating the Shimbunshi Jōrei (see Mitchell, *Censorship in Imperial Japan,* 46 ff.).

touch them with my hand, the cold shot through my body. Into the gloom came only half-light from the small opening of a window set so high that you could not reach it no matter how you stretched. There were thin mats spread out on the board floor to sit on, but they felt clammy with moisture.

I did as I was ordered, and sat down facing the entrance on a mat near the door. The door had iron plates at the top and bottom with iron grating in the middle. The guard had his table set up precisely facing me. Always to be under observation thus was unpleasant—peculiarly unpleasant even though the face of the guard was quite ordinary and not especially evil-looking. I remembered the Russian proverb, He who lives in a house of stone has a cold heart, and thought that without question the guard staring at me was a man with a cold heart.

As I was thinking this, the noise of some commotion came from the corridor and the guard opened the door, saying, "Come on." Beyond the door I saw about twenty convicts sitting on the concrete floor facing one another in two rows. Each had both hands placed on his knees and faced a food tray. I sat down at one end.

"Bow!" A loud voice gave an order that for a moment I did not understand. Everyone bent his head while keeping his hands on his knees. "Commence the meal!"

The loud voice ordered again, and again I didn't understand at first, hearing only "meal." Each immediately took up rice bowl and chopsticks. Then, in a great hurry, all began to rake in the rice from the single large hardened ball that had been placed in the center of each bowl. This is what must be meant, I thought, when people talk about "hungry ghosts." The men would separate some rice from the ball, shovel it into their mouths, swallow it, shovel again, swallow again. The pace was literally without a break. I was astounded by what I was watching.

The guard again shouted something. "Number 0000!" Startled, I turned toward the guard. "What are you staring at! Hurry up and eat!" he shouted at me.

I glanced down at my front and for the first time realized that my family name had become Number 0000. I quickly picked up my bowl. But before I could shovel in much more than about half of my ball of rice the rest of them were once again sitting straight up with hands on their knees.

From beginning to end, each time I saw this I never ceased to be amazed at how fast convicts ate their food. They raked it in and swallowed it down without ever using their teeth to chew anything.

A priest serving as the prison chaplain once said, knitting up his eyebrows the way priests do, "There is really nothing that can be done about it. No matter how often you tell them how harmful it is to the body, that's the way they do it. The reasons they give you are nonsense. It makes you pity them. Unless they chew well there is no way that it can be digested before passing through the stomach."

Moreover, it made me rather uncomfortable not to be finished when the others were sitting at attention and yawning while waiting for me. Nor could I deal with the so-called 40–60 rice—four parts Chinese rice and six parts barley with lots of unhulled particles. So I just put down my chopsticks.

We all filed back into the cells. I had been feeling quite forlorn but the meal revived my usual curiosity. According to our colleague Sakai, who had first been put in here some years before, at the physical examination they gave you on arrival they would have you get down on all fours naked while they peered up your anus. And when you walked you had to hold both arms down at your sides without moving them at all. The fact that these rules had been abolished left me feeling disappointed.

The place I have just been describing was a special section to hold those being punished with solitary confinement, or for temporarily holding new arrivals, or men on the eve of being released. The next morning I was immediately moved in with the semi-invalids and cripples I mentioned earlier.

Ishikawa Sanshirō[19] and Yamaguchi, who had both been convicted of violating the Press Ordinances, were also residents in this same section. I was put into a neighboring cell—first Ishikawa, then Yamaguchi, then me, in that order. It was a large room: twelve feet long by ten or

19. For more on Ishikawa, see chapter 6 part 6.

twelve feet wide, as I remember it. At the front and rear were the iron
gratings from the old lockup, but the rear grating was fitted with a large
sliding screen. When the screen was open you could see the spreading
branches of a large paulownia tree immediately outside the back grate.
Out the front grate, beyond a dirt floor about three feet wide, was another sliding screen. On the other side of that screen was another paulownia tree. To the left and to the right, separated by wooden doors,
other cells were laid out in the same way. The guard walked up and
down the dirt floor area.

I sat on one corner of the thin mat near the dirt floor area and stared
at the grate in front of my face. Aha, grating. Just as I expected! I
thought to myself, remembering what Sakai had described. This was
where he had been that time. He had been put in with a teacher and an
official from the textbook case.[20] For small men it might not be too bad
to be thus secluded together but I could see that it was an exceedingly
bad idea to put very many in there. The grating resembled that seen on
the windows of whorehouses and we resembled whores even though,
with our hairy faces, you would have to say that we were in the style of
intellectual prostitutes.[21] The guards resembled customers engaged in
window-shopping, and we would amuse ourselves by joking with them:
"Hello, you—the gentleman with the eyeglasses—please step in."

Once I became one of these *intellectual prostitutes,* my mood light-
ened. The cells were bright and we were usually allowed to see outside.
The sliding screens gave you the surprising feeling of being *at home.*
Right next door were my friends. Since the guards had to deal with
semi-invalids and cripples, they seemed to have been chosen for their
Buddha-like temperament.

Within an hour after I had been transferred to this cell, an inmate
suddenly stopped in front of my cell and stood staring at my face. I

20. A huge scandal beginning in 1902 over bribery in the sales of textbooks to
elementary schools involved more than 150 individuals. This paragraph also has a pun
about leading an idle life that does not translate well into English.

21. In the licensed quarters prostitutes were displayed behind grated windows. The
words in italics are an English gloss for the Chinese characters meaning "bearded
prostitute" and involve puns that are not fully translatable.

stared back, thinking his was a face I also should recognize but at first was not able to.

"What in the world are you doing in such a place?"

"Huh?"

"So, it *is* you! As I passed back and forth I was thinking your face was familiar and decided to ask."

He put on a sorrowful expression and spoke as if he found something incomprehensible. I myself found it not the least bit incomprehensible that *I* should be in a place like this. What I found incomprehensible was that I would meet *this* fellow in a place like this.

"I'm in on a press violation. Why are you?"

When I asked him what his crime had been, he turned bright red. "There's really nothing I can justify. But I just wanted to see if it was really you. Excuse me now; until another time." And then he rushed off.

He was a friend who had been expelled from military cadet school for reasons similar to those in my case. He had been at the cadet school in Sendai and I at the one in Nagoya but we both had been ordered out at almost the same time, just a half-year before graduation. Soon after that we met again by accident in Tokyo. Two other friends of his had been thrown out of Sendai with him. One had been a childhood friend of mine since elementary school. The four of us had fallen in together as fellow refugees from military school. Soon there were eight or nine in the group, including refugees from Osaka and Tokyo. We pulled together and made a pledge to study hard in order to wash away the shame of being expelled. We all were admitted to the fifth level in one or another middle school. Midway through, however, this fellow and another friend had broken their pledge and begun to play about. Indignant, we repeatedly admonished the two. Finally we announced that we were severing relations with them. The next year all the others passed the entrance examinations at various colleges, but none of us knew where or what these two were doing and all regretted having broken off contact.

Now it was four or five years later. I decided that whatever had landed him in jail must have happened just after we broke off contact and that was why he was surprised to see me here. I learned that he had a run-in with the principal of a school for delinquent boys in the Waseda district. He had done something more as a prank than as a serious crime but the school staff had termed him an accomplice in a larceny. Thus this erstwhile prodigy of the Sendai Military Cadet School was now in Sugamo Prison where he worked at such chores as bringing food to the other prisoners or carrying about work materials.

He worked at such chores until near the end of my second sentence. Where he got hold of them I don't know, but for a while he brought me lumps of rock salt almost every day. And each time he seemed to find out when it was the day for my wife's monthly visit and would come to inform me. "Your wife is here and the guard will be calling you any minute now, so please be ready."

Then one day he suddenly disappeared. But that night I received through a guard a note saying, "Tomorrow I'll be out on probation. Let's meet as soon as you get out." Yet I never saw him again.

There was another man, an old fellow over sixty, who also worked at chores. Just before I finished my second sentence this man too was released. He had served twenty-five or twenty-six years without being on the outside. One day when he was gazing at the light bulb as if in a trance he said, "No matter how much I hear about it I really cannot imagine such things as streetcars. The first time I found out about electric lights was in here."

Whenever a guard was there this man used to talk about all sorts of things. If there was no guard, however, he would seldom open his mouth unless it was relevant to his chores. This was true even when he was in his cell. While the rest waited for the guard to be on break in order to chatter away or play some joke, he would silently sit by himself reading a book printed with phonetic spelling. Even if you said something to him, he would not respond. Even when he was doing his chores, he was as stubborn as the most ill-tempered guard. Once when this old man brought me a change of clothes I complained.

"Hey, what am I supposed to do with a kimono as dirty as this? Couldn't you bring me a cleaner one?"

"They said it was laundered," he answered and moved on toward the next cell.

"Hey, you! Hey!" I shouted after him.

The guard heard me and came over and after listening to my griev-
ance he told the old man, "Go get him a new one." Mumbling under his
breath, the old man went to exchange it.

That wasn't the best example of this old man's stubbornness, but it
was always in the same mode. He took no notice of the complaints of
his fellow convicts. Every day we were allotted one small sheet of toilet
paper per person. When we had trouble with our bowels we would ask
for another piece, but never once would he exceed that one piece. Once
he even invoked the prison regulations against a guard who tried to tell
him to do something. For him, as I said, there was no leeway in following the rules. Those prison regulations were his avatars. He would
walk with arms motionless at his sides, the five fingers of each hand
pointed just so at the hips, as the rules of some years earlier used to
specify. Fixed on his sleeve were three square white merit badges.

In the beginning he had been condemned to death as a murderer, but
then that sentence was commuted to life and by some mechanism reduced and then reduced again. I heard he finally ended up being pardoned. He had been a stubborn man from the outset but stubborn also
in the sense of being honest. He regretted his crime, which had been the
result of stubbornness, and since coming into prison he had focused that
stubbornness entirely on the minute observance of prison regulations. In
a curious way he apparently became an even more stubborn man.

In the next cell were ten cripples. One was in his seventies. Another
was a young man with a face like one you would see on a chimpanzee
in the jungle. Another was a youth who limped along dragging his
strangely twisted body. Chimpanzee was not completely blind but was
apparently unable to see well out of either eye. He had a low forehead
with very narrow and ugly sunken eyes that were constantly blinking.
He got out once during my time there but soon came right back. All
these men seemed to be nothing but petty thieves.

The youth was a comedian. He kept everyone laughing uproariously
all day long. Someone would fart and he would begin to coax him as
you would a baby having a bowel movement, grunting and saying,
"That's good; come on now." Then everyone would fart over and over

again throughout the day and each time this fellow would say the same thing and get them all laughing. Sometimes even I would burst forth next door. When work became tiresome we would often go off to the toilet to take a break. If a guard came around two or three times and saw the same man on the toilet, he would reprimand him. Then this youth would reply, "This is a difficult delivery" and begin to grunt. Everyone would burst out laughing and the guard would have no choice but to say something like "All right, that's enough" and leave. It can't be measured how much this laughing from next door relieved my boredom over a long day.

My daily routine started every morning with cleaning the room as soon as I awoke. Then I could spend the whole day at the table reading, writing, or just thinking. In addition to a dictionary, I was allowed to keep five or six books at a time and every week I could exchange them for new ones. I was also given the privilege of having pen, ink, and paper. In order to show how I felt about this life, I will quote two or three letters I wrote at the time. All are from the early period.

> It's gotten hot, hasn't it. But we are in cell block #11, which they say is the coolest part of the prison. The brick walls, iron-plated doors, and three-foot windows make it different from the other cells. The whole southwestern wall is grating with three-inch-square strips and, moreover, both sides open directly to the outside. When the wind blows it is actually chilly. I am the only occupant in this 12' × 12' room. I sleep under a large old-fashioned mosquito net. These are rather luxurious accommodations for the son of a commoner. For clothing we receive two almost new kimonos and use one to sleep in. From time to time they are laundered.
>
> At the end of the next to last section in Lao Tzu is described a passively anarchical society: "*[Let the people be] contented with their food, pleased with their clothing, satisfied with their houses, and happy with their customs. Though there be a neighboring country in sight, and the people hear each other's cocks crowing and dogs barking, they would grow old and die without having anything to do with each other.*"[22] Our present life is

---

22. Ōsugi quotes from the *Tao-te Ching*, part of the canon of Taoist philosophy. This translation follows that given in William Theodore de Bary et al., *Sources of Chinese Tradition*, 63–64.

exactly like that except I would quibble with the part about being con-
tented with the food. Curiously, any sense that prison life is something
out of the ordinary has almost disappeared with me these days.
(to Sakai)

As I think about those mosquito nets now, I remember one night
when it was so hot that no one could sleep, one of the guards who were
strolling up and down stopped to make a comment.

"For you men it doesn't matter if it turns a bit hot. I have been pon-
dering this as I watch you all lying down under those mosquito nets. As
I watch you through the grating I no longer understand which of us is
the real prisoner!"

I also wrote a letter to Kōtoku.

> The heat of summer is passing. The evenings grow cool. Now I am on
> a joking basis with the guards, teasing them about getting fat and the like.
>
> Recently I have been doing a lot of reading and have noticed some-
> thing exceedingly interesting in the books by the anarchists Bakunin, Kro-
> potkin, Reclus, and Malatesta.[23] They and the other anarchists all start by
> discussing astronomy. Then they expound on biology. Then they finally
> discourse on human society. As I tire of reading and raise my head to gaze
> outside, the first things I see are the heavenly bodies, the movement of the
> clouds, the leaves of the paulownia tree, sparrows, black kites, crows; and
> then, lowering my gaze, the roof of the cell block across the way. It is
> exactly as if I were reviewing in practice what I was just reading. I am
> always ashamed at how very shallow my knowledge of nature is, so from
> now on I have decided to try to study nature fully.
>
> The more I read and the more I think about it, after all, nature is logic.
> Logic is completely realized amidst nature. Furthermore, in the same
> sense logic must be completely realized amidst the human societies that
> have developed in nature.
>
> Along with this resolve to study nature, at the same time my mind is
> powerfully attracted toward anthropology and human history. In this
> way, my desire to learn is like a spring bubbling over simultaneously in all
> directions . . . (abbreviated).[24]

23. Ōsugi refers to the Russian anarchists Mikhail Bakunin (1814–1876) and Pyotr
Kropotkin (1842–1921), the Frenchman Jean-Jacques Reclus (1830–1905), and the
Italian Enrico Malatesta (1858–1932).

24. The unexplained abbreviation is likely Ōsugi's.

How is your health? How is *Conquest of Bread* coming?[25] As soon as
I get out of prison, I would like to do Kropotkin's autobiography as I have
long desired. I am now deep into reading it.

There is also a letter I wrote to Yamakawa closer to the time when
I would be leaving prison. Some of it is about my appearance in court.
Toward the end are things about my hearing on the charge of violating
the Press Ordinances.

Yesterday I returned from Tokyo Jail. The first thing I did after entering my cell was to sit down at my table. I had the real feeling I had
come back home.

I hate going to court. I especially detest the continual questioning by
the judge. I wonder if it wouldn't be more satisfying if they were simply
honest and said, as in Russia, that they were going to send you straight to
Siberia without a trial—the ways of a strumpet are better than those of a
fine lady.

After court was over, I was taken straight to Tokyo Jail. As soon as I
enter the gate I always shudder at the thought of the bedbugs. In one night
I was bitten in no fewer than twenty-three places. With the stings and
itching I couldn't sleep a wink. When I returned to Sugamo after several
days all my prison friends went out of their way to ask after my health,
saying I looked too thin.

The only thing interesting about Tokyo Jail is the pigeons. Just when
it's meal time, they come beating their wings outside the window, calling
out in their strange way. I tried tossing them a small lump of rice. Ten
pigeons came swooping down and finished it off in no time. I tossed some
more. It was so fascinating I continued to do it over and over. I ended up
feeding them my whole breakfast down to the broth. Afterwards I was
very hungry, but it had been fascinating.

When I returned to Sugamo, the guards were solicitous, asking me:
"That was fast. What happened in court?" Somehow it put my mind at
rest. I felt as if I had come home.

However, this will not be my home for much longer. My long *inac-
tive*[26] life is also ending. I want to get out. I want to become very active.
I have given a great deal of thought to such activity. I have also made
some resolutions. Once out, I will discuss this at length with you all.
Please give my regards to all our comrades.

25. Between 1906 and 1908 Kōtoku worked on a translation of this work by
Kropotkin.
26. The word in italics is in English in the original.

I was out only for a month and a half. The next time I was put back
in it was together with Sakai, Yamakawa, and three other friends for the
Rooftop Speech Incident mentioned earlier. Once convicted, the other
three men were left in Tokyo Jail but Sakai, Yamakawa, and I were
brought back to Sugamo. The guards and prison friends all welcomed
me: "So you're back!"

I began a letter I wrote to Morichika Unpei with the following paragraph:

> I have been taken in again! But this time I am fortunate because I have
> come back before I had completely cleared my head of prison and I am
> accustomed to everything.

At the time Morichika was the editor of my newspaper, the *Japan Commoners News,* and later was executed along with Kōtoku and the others.[27]

Yamaguchi was sick with something and was in the infirmary. I am
certain that Yamakawa was placed in some other building. Ishikawa, I,
and Sakai, in that order, were neighbors. Ishikawa and I continued to
join in the pranks but Sakai lost the spirit of previous years when he too
had grasped the grating and called out, "Hello, you—the gentleman
with the beard!"

We found a nail while outside exercising and used it to make a hole
in the wall separating our cells. When bored with reading and taking
notes, one of us would call to the other through the hole. I would put
my ear to it while Ishikawa spoke, and then Ishikawa would put his ear
to the hole while I spoke. This didn't work very well. Often both would
have an ear or a mouth to the hole at the same time. How could we deal
with this, I wondered; one should first peer through to see if the other's
ear was waiting. But in the midst of our theorizing, we would both be
saying, "It's my turn to talk; you listen to me!" and my spittle would fly
past his through that tiny hole. Sometimes we would call through the
hole: "Hey, watch this!" and then back off to the center of the room to
put on a dance.

27. Morichika Unpei (1881–1911) trained in agricultural science before becoming an
activist and was, like Ōsugi, close to Kōtoku as well as Sakai.

While we were at this sort of thing, Ishikawa was writing a nearly two-thousand-page *History of Social Movements in the West*. Its publication was later banned. Sakai and I were translating for a series of books being edited by Sakai under the title *Science for Commoners*. Yamakawa was also involved in that project.

Then, just as we had each completed one volume, Sakai, Yamakawa, and I finished our time. Sakai and I told Ishikawa: "It's a pity, but you'll have to play the role of Shunkan on Kikaigashima.[28] But it will only be a bit longer. Be patient!" As we left the building we called out, "Hey, Shunkan—goodbye!"

III. CHIBA

But before a half-year had passed I was hauled from the scene of the Red Flags Incident to Tokyo Jail and charged under the fancy designation of Obstructing Officials and Violation of the Peace Preservation Law. There were twelve of us including Sakai, Yamakawa, Arahata,[29] me, and four of our women comrades. The women were not convicted because the police gave poor testimony, but one of them was Kanno Sugako who would later start a magazine with Kōtoku, be arrested for violating the Press Laws, and eventually be executed with Kōtoku.

This was in the midst of the trials on the Streetcar Fare Incident of two years before. There were seven or eight in this group—including Nishikawa and Yamaguchi—whose cases like mine spanned both incidents. At the first trial we had been found innocent and, after the procurator appealed, the case had been dismissed again. But they had appealed it to the Supreme Court, which soon ordered a retrial in the Sendai Appellate Court that then found us guilty. Therefore, at that time we were out on bail during the Supreme Court proceedings. Bail was immediately cancelled and we were imprisoned at Tokyo Jail.

28. Shunkan was a twelfth-century Buddhist priest banished to the island of Kikaigashima after an attempted coup d'état but not released from exile when his two co-conspirators were pardoned. Over the centuries the story inspired a number of plays well known in Japanese theater.

29. Arahata Kanson (1887–1981) was later a co-founder of the Japanese Communist party.

Tokyo Jail was full of friends. Since all except the women were found guilty, there was not room enough for us all to be held in single cells. Yet since we were viewed as if we were carriers of some plague germs it wouldn't do either to put us in with the other convicts or to house us together with our friends for fear that the infection would become more virulent. Therefore they transferred every one of us to new-style facilities at Chiba Prison, which had the reputation of being a model prison because it was the only one in Japan where the system was based on single cells.

The guard in charge of the transportation escort bragged about the place in the tones of an uncle who was bringing a nephew to his house for the first time. (In fact, from start to finish this guard was like a kind uncle to us.) The prison was built in a good location on a rise in the northern suburbs of Chiba. It is said that the temperature in the winter in Chiba was about five degrees centigrade higher than in Tokyo. If so, then the temperature in Chiba Prison must be five degrees higher than the town. In the same fashion, the summers were cooler. As the train neared Chiba, he pointed out the left-hand window of our car.

"There it is—where you're all going."

We peered out at it. There we could see its splendid beauty, surrounded by a tall brick wall and shining radiantly in the sunlight of a lovely September day. When I saw it on a cloudy day or in the rain, the color of the building, which made me think of a persimmon-colored kimono I had seen somewhere, produced an odd melancholy in me. Yet when the sun was shining, it mysteriously lifted my spirits.

"It makes me hungry for sardines!"

Arahata, who was sitting right next to me, had got one of the trusties to purchase some for him just the day before. No matter how often we went to jail, the accent was always on salted cod or salmon or some other kind of fish. Hearing him, I begin to feel a singularly pleasurable anticipation: "That's it! I want to hurry up and get there to eat."

Arahata and several others sitting there began to laugh happily.

When we arrived we saw that the newly constructed building sparkled. The brick-walled cells were about four and a half mats in size and, facing south, brightly lit. The first thing you noticed was the large window. It was as pleasant as the Tokyo hospital room I once stayed in.

From the outset, however, I was shocked at the lack of sense on the part of the officers. On our arrival they lined us up and made us take instruction from the head of the intake unit. Over and over again he said, in effect: "All of you have been given long sentences, but if you intend to observe carefully the prison rules, then those on two-year sentences can be out in one, those on one-year can be out in six months."

We sneered at him, thinking what a hoax it was. Moreover, even if I had thought he meant well by telling us this, he was half-witted to think he could do us favors such as getting us paroles. We didn't believe any of it. If that had been all, it would have been all right. But after they finished with the instructions, one by one they took the row of eight (those of us from the streetcar incident were lined up in front) into the next room. There the officer's words were more cold.

"You've done some very stupid things. We say that once you are in here you get what is coming to you. Each of you is going to."

He treated us as if we were thugs for some political party. As you might expect, all it did was make everyone from Sakai on down look at one another and smile grimly. Arahata habitually bit his nails out of nervousness, but ever since he entered prison he exhibited a cheerfulness that was a complete reversal. Now he let out a loud laugh, "Ha ha!" The guard gave a puzzled look.

The annoying thing was that almost all the officers from the warden down to the guards adopted the same tone. Furthermore, though we had been hoping for sardines, what came for supper was miso soup with eggplant leaves. For breakfast the next day we had the identical miso soup with eggplant leaves. At lunch it got more unbearable: there were two slices of pickled radish with sesame salt.

Moreover, the stipulations of imprisonment were different than before in that they imposed a fixed amount of labor as penal servitude. The work at Tokyo Jail had involved making things out of clean pieces of wood and had been easy. Here it was tougher. We twisted together lengths of Chinese hemp to make the core of thongs for wooden clogs. Your hands got chapped, and if you were not careful they were rubbed raw. It was dusty. It was taxing. It lasted ten hours in the daytime and on top of that they gave us two or three hours of night work. I had enough after the very first day.

On the third or fourth day I woke up with a start at the voice of a guard, "Hey, get up!" I had been doing this every day almost nonstop and was worn out from the work. I was so sleepy I couldn't keep my eyes open. Seated in my cell during the thirty-minute rest break following another luncheon of sesame salt, I kept nodding off. At some point I slid on my side without waking and was lying on top of a quilt.

"Lazybones! What are you doing—sleeping right in the middle of the day? Say, don't you care anything about the prison regulations?"

With that bullying tone, the guard was showing how tough he was on roughnecks like me. Shortly later I was called to the warden's office. On the way there I prepared an apology: I was weak and had been exhausted because I was not accustomed to the work. But no sooner did I enter the warden's office than without any preamble he began to rail at me ferociously.

"You socialists! You think you can just come in here and ignore our prison regulations. I'm putting you on reduced rations. And if I ever see you break the rules again, I won't stop with reducing your rations!"

It reminded me of the father of a schoolmate at the Foreign Language School, a vice admiral in the navy I think, who was notorious for his short temper and tongue-lashings. (The warden even looked enough like my friend's father to be him.) I had to stifle a laugh at the absurd tone of his railing:

"All right. Whatever you say."

"What!" The warden swiveled in his chair so that he was facing me directly. I remained silently smiling back. He then shouted at the guard standing at attention behind me.

"Take him back!"

I did a sharp about-face just as I had been taught in cadet school and marched out of the warden's office. It was the custom whenever we were scolded in cadet school and this time, without thinking or intending any sarcasm, I reverted to my old habit.

There was another curious habit from cadet school days that I also rediscovered in prison. It would often happen that I was called to the office of the captain of the guard to be berated about something. That guard was a short pudgy hunchbacked fellow with a bushy beard. In the midst of his hairy face were narrow eyes that seemed to glitter with malice. We called him the bear. The room was in the Western-style brick building and was furnished with tables and chairs. Thus he had his shoes on and was seated in a chair, but there were two thin mats placed on the dusty floor. As I entered he pointed with his chin to them.

"Sit over there."

I was irate but remained silent, as if I didn't understand him.

"Why aren't you sitting?"

"I don't feel like sitting there."

"Why not?"

"We can talk with me standing, can't we?"

"I don't have to argue with you! Sit down!"

"I'll sit there if you'll sit there."

Hearing that reply, the guard screwed up his hairy brow, sprang to his feet, and shouted.

"Sit! That's an order!"

Instantaneously, as the word "order" reached my ears, I felt as if my whole body was struck by some overwhelming force. In the same instant I felt seized against my will by a rebellious spirit. My usual attitude, which would have led me simply to sneer back, immediately changed into defiance and I answered him.

"What do you mean, *order?* If you want to make me sit, go ahead and make me sit."

This time—just as earlier in the warden's office—I was simply sent back to my cell. Nothing was said of whatever it was that I was supposed to be reprimanded about.[30]

30. Significant in the cultural context of this confrontation over sitting is the fact that the status differential symbolized here was unequivocal subordination but not necessarily abject subjugation; in an 1898 strike, railway engineers and firemen complained about a similar sitting arrangement vis-à-vis assistant stationmasters (Stephen E. Marsland, *The Birth of the Japanese Labor Movement,* 91).

The habit of cowering at the word "order" has become engrained over thousands of years of slavery, but in my case I suppose it is more the spiritual relic of military cadet school. Basically I am an extremely weak man. If at times I have appeared to be strong, that appearance of strength has been a bluff that stemmed from my vanity. Nothing wounds my vanity more than revealing my own weakness. I cannot bear such wounds in silence. Whether I truly had strength or not, I would bluff and make it seem strength both to the other man and to myself. At times I wonder whether my whole self consists of such vanity.

They said that if I broke the rules again they wouldn't stop with cutting my food ration. But there were two subsequent occasions when my ration was reduced, once for three days and once for five days. The first time I was caught talking in the exercise yard with Arahata and we both were punished. I don't remember now what the second time was about.

Like me, Arahata was often reprimanded. He recounted one incident to me, laughing loudly as he told me. One evening when the moon was unusually beautiful, they caught him up standing under the window and gazing out.

"What're you doing there, gawking? . . . Hey, what do you mean, looking at the moon? You're stupid—what's there to see in the moon?"

Such, in essence, is how we were treated at the beginning of our stay in prison. Yet no matter how the other side treated us, somehow we had to turn those long prison terms of one and two years to our own benefit. I racked my brain over this for about two weeks. The one best method was reading and contemplation. What was needed was a decision about the direction of that reading and contemplation.

From the very beginning I resolved: one crime, one language. By that I meant I would study another foreign language each time I was jailed. The first time while waiting for the verdict I did Esperanto. Then in Sugamo I did Italian. The second time in Sugamo I nibbled a bit at German. Awaiting conviction this time, I again started in on German. But since the sentence was such a long one, I decided that once I had done German for a while I would try Russian. I also wanted to try a bit of Spanish. I knew from past experience that I could get through the rudiments in three months and after six months would be able to read quite a bit without a dictionary. Thus I could do a language each year. I decided that the afternoon would be my language period.

Saying this makes me sound like a distinguished scholar of linguistics. Actually, I succeeded in sticking to my plan and got to the point that I could boast some. But afterward I grew very lazy and, since I no longer attend even the academy of prison, it has all gone to waste.

I also decided that during these two and a half years I would realize my long-held ambition to become a specialist in sociology. But to study the type of sociology that then existed would be of no value. I had my heart set on pursuing my own kind of sociology. First, I would master the essentials of biology in order to discover the fundamental characteristics of human beings who organized themselves into societies. Next, in order to know the stages by which humans came to conduct life as humans in societies, I would proceed to anthropology, especially comparative anthropology. Following that, I would try to arrive at a sociology built on the basis of these two sciences. Thinking about it now causes me real embarrassment—those were the ideas of a mere novice. As I added this or that book to those that I wanted to read and then tried to calculate how many days it would take to read them, there was no way that two and a half years would be enough. I would want at least another half-year. Thus the two and a half years that until then I had thought would be so long suddenly became inadequate. I began to give serious thought to how I might manage to get the time lengthened by another half-year.

There was the work to be done. But once you became used to it, it wasn't so much. The number of sandals to be done each day was set at one hundred; but if you did half of that amount, or a fourth, or even less, it was all right. Whatever you were told, you could stubbornly refuse to do more. The secret was that all the prisoners conferred and agreed among themselves to set a limit. Actually, that agreement came about naturally almost from the start. In any event, I stole time from work to study whenever I could.[31]

---

31. Incongruous as this leniency seems, Ōsugi's comrades report similar opportunities for study; see Thomas Duane Swift, "Yamakawa Hitoshi," 114. Since Yamakawa's health suffered greatly in prison, his accounts are bleaker than Ōsugi's.

Once I determined this, I read avidly. As I grew used to the work, I performed it faster and faster. We got them to substitute superior Japanese hemp for the inferior Chinese hemp. The work became increasingly easier. Yet the amount of work I completed never increased. Instead I waited for a time when I was not being watched and then did my reading.

Thus I almost completely discarded the teachings I had previously assembled so avidly and now undertook to reconstruct my head all over again.

As my enthusiasm for scholarship flourished, my appetite for food grew apace—or rather, I should say it was shocking how vulgarly gluttonous I became. The first time I was in Tokyo Jail we could have food sent in from outside, so there was no problem. During the first and even the second time in Sugamo, the sentences were short, so the problem was not that great. But this time it got so bad that I was disgusted with myself. Once I had been very finicky about what I ate; now it no longer mattered what I put in my mouth. The foul-tasting 40–60 rice—a third to a half of which I used to leave in my bowl—I now dispatched completely, leaving literally not a single grain behind. Meticulously I would ferret out, poke at, and gather in every morsel that had stuck to the side of the rice tub or rice ladle, even the morsel that had fallen free. Whether today's lump of rice—which had been measured out precisely so much for each portion and carefully shaped just so into a ball—was larger or smaller than yesterday's was a cause for secret rejoicing or cursing. As the guard ladled out the broth we strained our eyes and cocked our ears in order to tell whether the dipper struck the bottom of the bucket. If it reached clear down to the bottom it would bring up more. The top of the box the meals came in served as a tray. We placed our bowls on it to receive our ration of broth. Some of the broth spilled onto that tray; each meal one of us took his turn to get the collected leftover broth by tilting that cover. I cannot tell you how impatiently I waited for my turn to come.

Whenever I came across a passage about food in the novels I was reading, I would flip the pages to skip those passages. I couldn't bear to read about it. Even when I was reading or thinking about something else, suddenly without warning it would become associated with food.

Occasionally I dreamed about food. I heard that Sakai too often had such dreams. For him it was always a feast of delicacies from the Sankai region that appeared. Yet whenever Sakai would reach out with his chopsticks, some hindrance would intervene to prevent him from eating and he would be cruelly disappointed. My dream, by contrast, would be very paltry. I would be passing a shop in which a great variety of sweets and cakes were displayed. Unable to hold myself back, I would charge in and gobble them up one after another, straining to stuff down more until my throat as well as my stomach was full. The mysterious thing was that I would then wake up ill and writhing in pain. I would dash full tilt to the toilet; if I did not, then after I got up the next day I had diarrhea. It is hard to believe.

Sexual desire was another exceedingly odd matter. While I was in Tokyo Jail or Sugamo, I would have unexpected urges from time to time. That never happened at all after I arrived here. When I was young I thought that hermits or prelates who could suppress their sexual desires were admirable, but as I grew older I decided that if such humans existed, it was because in their dotage they had become impotent. Both views, however, are mistaken. I am a mortal so lowly that I can stuff myself in a dream to the point that it makes me awaken with diarrhea. Yet in certain times and circumstances I could turn into a saintly being or superior man without arduous practice or mortification. Some nights, fearing that perhaps I had become impotent, I would purposely fantasize or try to recall specific situations. But none of these memories or fantasies came alive. I was almost in despair.

One year of my sentence finally passed. Then another year passed, and I stayed behind as Sakai and Yamaguchi finished their two-year terms. Suddenly someone from the procurator's office arrived. He spoke in vague terms, inquiring whether I knew that some of my friends had been up to something serious—as serious as it could be—and that Kōtoku and many others had been arrested.[32] If I knew only that, how did

---

32. In spring 1910 hundreds of left-wing activists were interrogated about a plot to assassinate the emperor. Of the twenty-six convicted at least three were close to Ōsugi: Kōtoku Shūsui, Kanno Sugako, and Morichika Unpei; see Fred G. Notehelfer, "High Treason Incident of 1910."

I know even that much? He said he was just making a routine inquiry, but it smelled suspicious to me and I made up some answers.

A few days passed and then unexpectedly I was hauled off to Tokyo Jail under tremendously heavy guard. From there I was called to the procurator's office and then I was formally interrogated concerning the so-called High Treason Incident. They tried to rattle me.

"Planning for this scheme started four or five years back. You can't tell us you didn't know anything about it. It's known from the confession of the other defendants that you were originally part of the plot."

I replied only that if I didn't know anything about any of it, then I didn't know anything.

Back in prison everyone, from the warden down to each one of the guards, strongly sympathized with me. One guard consoled me by speaking openly: "It's really too bad you've been dragged into this affair and have to go through all this trouble."

In the beginning I thought that the whole thing was a bit crazy; then, as all this sympathy was heaped on me, I began to feel more and more uneasy. I began to worry that if the prison staff took it so seriously, could it not be that the procurator's office really had decided we were all in on a conspiracy? I tried to allay these suspicions but I could tell from the expressions on the guards' faces that my effort wasn't working. I tried to resign myself—if that's how it's going to be, there's nothing more to be done about it. But I continued to be anxious as long as it was not clear whether that was how it was going to be.

Eventually Sakai finished his time and was released without any trouble. That relieved a good part of my uneasiness. But the prison staff's attitude toward me did not change. As my own term also neared an end, I thought I should make preparations for release. I asked for a waiver of the rules regarding letters and visits, usually allowed only once every two months. The warden and the captain of the guard would not even consider it, saying simply that such things were out of the question. They would only give me sympathetic looks. If there was no doubt in their minds, how could I doubt that I was to be included with the others? However, when the procurators did not examine me any further, I could allay some of the doubt.

In that period I saw almost all the defendants in the High Treason case. The entrance to the bath was right next to my cell and the outer corridor leading to and from the bath entrance stretched out in front of me for several dozen yards. Whenever I had a chance, I watched that corridor from my window. Each prisoner had his face hidden under large woven-straw headgear, yet those I knew I could recognize from their build and manner. I could also guess who the others were because they were brought under such extraordinarily tight guard.

One day I caught sight of Kōtoku passing by. "Hey, Kōtoku! Kōtoku!" I called to him two or three times but not in a very loud voice. (Today I regret what was probably stupid hesitation on my part.) Kōtoku was a little deaf and he went on without seeming to hear me.

Finally the day arrived when I had finished my time. The guards were extraordinarily pleasant as they took me to the gate at Tokyo Jail. Six or seven friends waited for me outside. We all shook hands.

All day long, the day of my release, I chatted on about things in prison but became mute the next day. I could hardly speak. Was it because of having gone for more than two years without conversation? Or was it because of the excitement of an abrupt change in my life, having left prison? In any case, the stuttering I had always suffered from suddenly became awful. It was so bad you could hardly even call it stuttering. For a whole month afterward I communicated almost entirely by writing. Whether at home or going out I was never without a pencil and piece of notepaper. Frequently I would be asked, "Can you hear?" Of course there was nothing wrong with my ears. When I wrote something down and handed it to people who did not know that, they too would write down their answer and hand it back to me.

This condition was not confined to me. A friend who had served a year on a charge of lèse-majesté was also a stutterer; the day after being released from prison he too became mute. For about a month he communicated by writing notes in the same way.

Something more commonplace also occurred. For a time before I got out I would dream about what I would eat on the outside and how much I would eat. But when I did get out everything I ate was extraordinarily delicious. Above all else was white rice. When I took up the bowl its whiteness seemed to form a shining halo. I put the rice in my mouth. My teeth seemed enveloped, as if I lay on a down-filled quilt under something pleasantly soft and at the same time was bathed in an intensely sweet broth that sprang from the end of my tongue. White rice by itself was enough. I wanted nothing else. When I reminisce with my comrades who are ex-convicts, we'll start to laugh and say, "Thinking about that still doesn't stop you from going to the lockup!" Still, only an ex-convict can fully savor Japanese rice.[33]

33. Ōsugi was taken into custody at least four more times after the publication of this section of his early prison experiences. On the last occasion, following the great Tokyo earthquake of September 1923, a Captain Amakasu of the military police killed Ōsugi, his wife Itō Noe, and her young nephew. For discussion of the murders and subsequent trial of Amakasu, see Stanley, *Ōsugi Sakae,* chap. 11.

BIBLIOGRAPHY

WORKS CITED IN THE NOTES

Arima, Tatsuo. *The Failure of Freedom: A Portrait of Modern Japanese Intellectuals.* Cambridge, Mass.: Harvard University Press, 1969.

Brown, Sidney Devere. "Political Assassination in Early Meiji Japan." In *Meiji Japan's Centennial: Aspects of Political Thought and Action,* ed. David Wurfel, 19–35. Lawrence: University Press of Kansas, 1971.

Cook, Theodore Failor, Jr. "The Japanese Officer Corps: The Making of a Military Elite, 1872–1945." Ph.D. dissertation, Princeton University, 1987.

Dai jinmei jiten (Biographical dictionary). 10 volumes. Tokyo: Heibonsha, 1957.

de Bary, William Theodore, Wing-tsit Chan, and Burton Watson, compilers, *Sources of Chinese Tradition.* New York: Columbia University Press, 1960.

Kenkyusha New Japanese-English Dictionary. 17th edition. Tokyo: Kenkyūsha, 1957.

Kinmonth, Earl H. *The Self-Made Man in Meiji Japanese Thought: From Samurai to Salary Man.* Berkeley: University of California Press, 1981.

Kodansha Encyclopedia of Japan. 9 volumes. Tokyo: Kodansha International, 1983.

Large, Stephen S. *Organized Workers and Socialist Politics in Interwar Japan.* Cambridge: Cambridge University Press, 1981.

Marshall, Byron K. Review of *Schooldays in Imperial Japan,* by Donald T. Roden. *Journal of Japanese Studies* 8, no. 1 (Winter 1982): 205–8.

Marsland, Stephen E. *The Birth of the Japanese Labor Movement.* Honolulu: University of Hawaii Press, 1989.

Mitchell, Richard H. *Censorship in Imperial Japan.* Princeton: Princeton University Press, 1983.

Notehelfer, Fred G. *Kōtoku Shūsui: Portrait of a Japanese Radical.* Cambridge: Cambridge University Press, 1971.

———. "Japan's First Pollution Incident." *Journal of Japanese Studies* 1, no. 2 (Spring 1975): 351–83.

———. "High Treason Incident of 1910." In *Kodansha Encyclopedia of Japan,* 3: 135–36. Tokyo: Kodansha International, 1983.

Ōsugi Sakae. *Ōsugi Sakae zenshū* (Complete works). 9 volumes. Tokyo: Ōsugi Sakae Zenshū Kankōsha, 1925–1928.

———. "Jijōden, Nihondatsu shukki." In *Gendai Nihon bungaku zenshū,* ed. Yamamoto Sansei, 39: 427–592. Tokyo: Kaizōsha, 1930.

———. "Jijōden, Nihondatsu shukki." In *Gendai Nihon bungaku zenshū,* 52: 47–134. Tokyo: Chikuma Shobō, 1957.

———. *Jijōden.* Tokyo: Gendai Shisō Sha, 1961.

Roden, Donald T. *Schooldays in Imperial Japan: A Study of the Culture of a Student Elite.* Berkeley: University of California Press, 1980.

Rubin, Jay. *Injurious to Public Morals: Writers and the Meiji State.* Seattle: University of Washington Press, 1984.

Stanley, Thomas A. *Ōsugi Sakae: Anarchist in Taishō Japan—the Creativity of the Ego.* Cambridge, Mass.: Harvard University Council on East Asian Studies, 1982.

Swift, Thomas Duane. "Yamakawa Hitoshi and the Dawn of Japanese Socialism." Ph.D. dissertation, University of California, Berkeley, 1970.

Totten, George O. *The Social Democratic Movement in Prewar Japan.* New Haven: Yale University Press, 1966.

Yamada Seizaburō, ed. *Puroretaria bungakushi: wakamo no jidai* (History of proletarian literature: its young era). Tokyo: Shakaimondai Kenkyūjo, 1953.

OTHER WORKS CONSULTED

Abe Isoh. "Socialism in Japan." In *Fifty Years of New Japan,* ed. Ōkuma Shigenobu, 2: 494–512. New York: Dutton & Co., 1909.

Akamatsu Katsumaro. *Nihon shakai undō no rekishiteki kenkyū* (Historical studies on the Japanese socialist movement). Tokyo: Romu Gyōsei, 1948.

Bernstein, Gail Lee. *Japanese Marxist: A Portrait of Kawakami Hajime.* Cambridge, Mass.: Harvard University Press, 1972.

Crump, John. *The Origins of Socialist Thought in Japan.* New York: St. Martin's Press, 1983.

Dictionnaire biographique du mouvement ouvrier international: le Japon. 2 volumes. Paris: Editions ouvrières, 1979.

Duus, Peter, and Irwin Scheiner. "Socialism, Liberalism and Marxism, 1901–1931." In *The Cambridge History of Modern Japan,* ed. Peter Duus, 6: 654–710. Cambridge: Cambridge University Press, 1988.

Eguchi Kyoshi. "Ōsugi Sakae—Arishima Takeo—Kagawa Toyohiko." *Chūōkōron* 70 (November 1955): 417–25.

Endō Iwau. "Minshūgeijutsu no mondai" (The question of art for the people). *Kokugo to kokubungaku* 32 (February 1955).

Hane, Mikiso. *Reflections on the Way to the Gallows: Voices of Japanese Rebel Women.* New York: Pantheon Books, 1988.

Katayama Sen. *The Labor Movement in Japan.* Chicago: Charles H. Kerr, 1918.

Kublin, Hyman. *Asian Revolutionary: The Life of Katayama Sen.* Princeton: Princeton University Press, 1964.

Large, Stephen S. "The Romance of Revolution in Japan: Anarchism and Communism during the Taishō Period." *Modern Asian Studies* 11, no. 3 (1977): 441–67.

Morito Tatsuo. "Ōsugi Sakae chosaku gairyaku" (A summary of the writings of Ōsugi Sakae). In *Ōsugi Sakae ikō,* ed. Yasutani Kan'ichi, 373–425. Tokyo: Kinseidō, 1928.

Nihon kindaishi jiten. Tokyo: Tōyō Keizai Shinpōsha, 1958.

Nihon rekishi daijiten. Tokyo: Kawade Shobō Shinsha, 1957.

Nishida Masaru. "Ōsugi Sakae nenpu" (Chronology of Ōsugi Sakae). In *Gendai Nihon bungaku zenshū,* 52: 424–28. Tokyo: Chikuma Shobō, 1957.

Ōsawa Masamichi. "Ōsugi Sakae ron" (On Ōsugi Sakae). *Shisō no kagaku* 21–23 (September–November 1960).

Scalapino, Robert A. *The Japanese Communist Movement, 1920–1966.* Berkeley: University of California Press, 1967.

Sievers, Sharon L. "Kōtoku Shūshui, *The Essence of Socialism:* A Translation and Bibliographical Essay." Ph.D. dissertation, Stanford University, 1969.

———. *Flowers in Salt: Beginnings of Feminist Consciousness in Modern Japan.* Stanford: Stanford University Press, 1983.

Smith, Henry Dewitt. *Japan's First Student Radicals.* Cambridge, Mass.: Harvard University Press, 1972.

Stone, Alan. "The Muckrakers." *Journal of Japanese Studies* 1, no. 2 (Spring 1975): 385–407.

U.S. War Department. *Japanese Military Dictionary: Japanese–English, English–Japanese.* Technical Manual 30–541. Washington, D.C.: Government Printing Office, 1944.

Yasutani Kan'ichi, ed. *Ōsugi Sakae ikō* (Articles by Ōsugi Sakae). Tokyo: Kinseidō, 1928.

Compositor: A-R Editions, Inc.
Text: 10/15 Sabon
Display: Monotype Van Dijck
Printer: Haddon Craftsmen, Inc.
Binder: Haddon Craftsmen, Inc.